BABY SLEEP

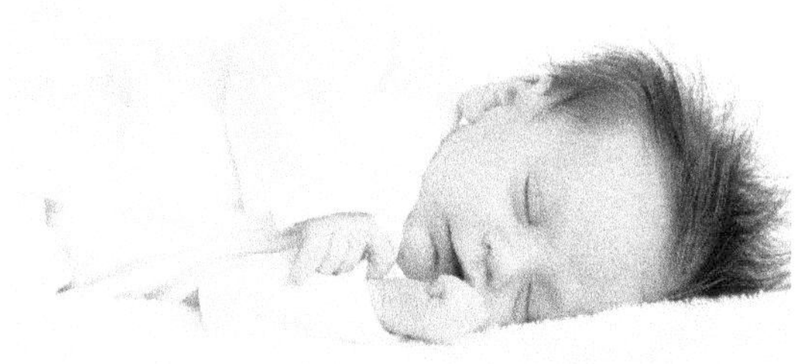

SLEEP TRAINING **TECHNIQUES** FOR A BABY OR TODDLER

A Modern Way to Improve the Sleep of Your Baby, Based Entirely on SCIENCE & INSTINCT

BE TRUE

I love U!

Contents

INTRODUCTION

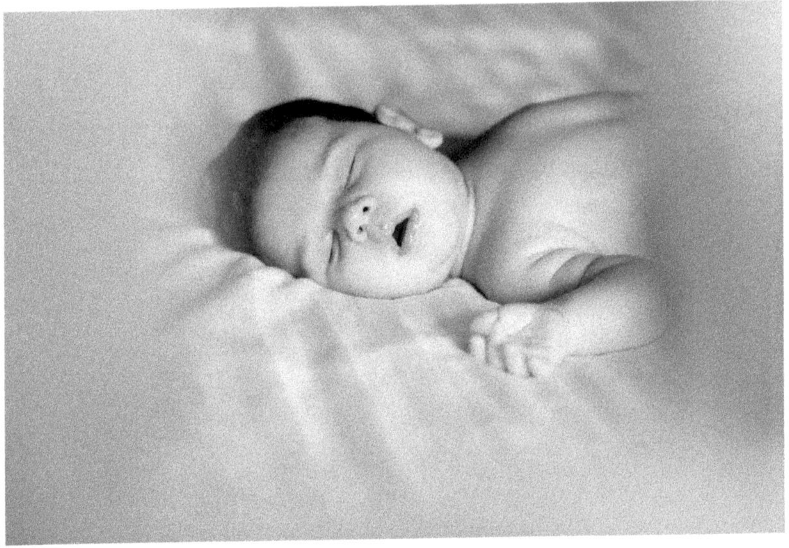

Do you remember when, waiting for the baby to be born, they repeated to you: ***"Sleep now, because later ... "***. It seemed like one of the many unsolicited comments and - come to think of it - it felt a bit like a jinx. ***Why should a child who does not sleep happen to me?***

Then the baby is born and the first month pass, in which one still feels charged enough not to expect rhythms and regularities. Then, little by little, it becomes clear that sleeping a whole night, without interruptions, is a distant memory. Is this happening to you too?

Is bedtime a family tragedy?

The baby does not want to go to sleep and takes an infinite time to fall asleep. Games and nursery rhymes are never enough. In the night he (and you) wakes up four-five-six-seven times. If everything goes well. If he doesn't have a bad dream. If he's not sick.

The result at the parental level is always the same: you end up in the evening like a zombie. Frightened. Nervous. Tired. And we realize that the sleep-deprived parent is willing to do anything to change the situation.

At this point a friend, or the kindergarten teacher, or the pediatrician or even a colleague moved to compassion, recommends that you read a manual that contains an easy way to put your children to bed.

Faced with this method, other parents are horrified and tell you that no, you will never, ever have to adopt it. Two models, two practices, two opposing ideologies. You don't know which one to choose (and you are right). Here they are explained.

The Estivill Model

A friend, or the kindergarten teacher, or even a colleague moved to compassion suggests you read "Take a nap", a superclassic for parents, written by the Catalan doctor Eduard

Estivill together with the journalist Sylvia de Béjar. The book offers practical advice for solving the problem of sleeping and, despite the great amount of criticism received, it is often recommended.

The basic idea is that "you learn to sleep", just as you learn to eat with a plate and cutlery. According to the authors, every baby, at six to seven months, is able to fall asleep on his own and sleep the whole night with the light off. What's more: he is able to go back to sleep without the need for external help in the case of nocturnal awakenings. It is enough for parents to have the right habits right from the start.

This technique, known among experts as the gradual quenching of crying or sleep training, has been heavily criticized as being too violent for the baby's psyche.

How do you teach a newborn to sleep? By creating a routine that precedes falling asleep and helping him to "count" only on objects that can remain at his disposal throughout the night.

It follows that it is above all objects that assume importance for the child, more than relationships, human warmth, the positive presence of an adult protector. To fall asleep, you just need the cradle, the teddy bear, the pacifier, the mobile, the blanket. The goal is autonomy: it is forbidden to lullaby, hold in one's arms, give a bottle, warm the tummy.

When it is time to put the child to bed (the recommended time is 8.30 pm) the very firm parents say goodnight. They turn off the light and walk away, without touching the baby any more.

Bedtime

If the child begins to call, if he cries and if he screams, the "method" says not to give in to the calls. Don't get your heart broken (but can you?). If the age already allows the child to get up, the suggestion is to "place barriers in front of the door".

After a minute of reminders, following a reassuring table, you can go back to the baby's room, stop for a moment and leave immediately. By continuing in this way, and progressively increasing the time spent away, the child is taught to remain alone.

The promise, in the end, is that the baby will learn to fall asleep on his own and we will all sleep happily ever after.

Sleeping with high contact

Unlike the Estivill method and decidedly sweeter and more fruitful, even at the level of humanity and feelings, there is the method of high-contact parenting.

Sweet dreams, recommended by the Leche League (the English name of the League for Breastfeeding), or "Let's sleep" are books whose approach is soft and flexible. At the heart of the model are parents who can learn to listen and respond to their children's needs in an intuitive way, without trying to adapt them to their rules.

The watchword is harmony. No preconceived idea, indeed, an invitation to rediscover one's individuality and one's intuitive role. But above all, an invitation to respect the child and trust him, so that he can in turn learn to trust us.

Slip into sleep without fear

Don't let him cry, because it is certainly not by force or neglect that the baby will learn to sleep. Leaving a child alone only means teaching him that there is no one who wants to listen to him when he is afraid, when he is hungry or thirsty. Listening to the child, on the other hand, means understanding that with crying (or with words, if he is older) he is able to communicate where he feels safe and where he is peaceful. Listen to him. You will see that he will show you the right accommodation. The one that will also allow you to sleep better.

In high contact parenting it may be helpful to adopt co-sleeping. In the bed next to their parents, children fall asleep faster and, if they wake up, they fall asleep again. If the child is afraid, you are always there and ready to reassure him, sometimes almost without waking up. You do not necessarily have to share the bed: you can sleep in the same room, or arrange a three-seater bed with a "side- bed cradle", or even put mattresses on the floor.

Which line to follow?

Between the "hard" and the sweet method, which one to choose? First of all, let's eliminate a prejudice. Many parents believe that all children except their own go to bed quietly without throwing a tantrum. Or that other people's children sleep all night without waking up. It is not so. Trust me.

Every night, children (all children) are cradled, pampered, brought to the bed, brought back to their bed and maybe even scolded. Sleep is linked to a thousand variables and there is no right recipe, suitable for everyone for every occasion.

Bedtime must be faced at the level of the family system. We proceed by trial and error and the best solution is to combine listening and observation. When, where and how do babies sleep well? Why do they sleep on some occasions and not on others?

By observing the answers, the right way is found to improve family strategies. A single reassuring fact: the quality of sleep naturally improves with growth. Sometimes you just need to wait a week, a month, two years. However, sleep problems are bound to resolve spontaneously.

Some good advice (which is good for everyone)

COMMON SENSE

To put a baby to sleep, be guided by common sense. A parent who can catch up on some sleep during the day may accept being a little more awake at night. But if all the adults in the family have to deal with a day of office or responsible jobs the next day, they'd better get enough rest at night. In this case, external help may be necessary, perhaps planning a few nights with grandparents (or other relatives or friends to whom you can ask). Or establish a shift system between both parents.

NO EXTREMISM

If you are attracted to a rigid "method", apply it with a little consistency but without extremes. For example: we insist that he get used to his room. All right. But we sit by and hold his hand, without setting up barriers or letting him cry for 17 minutes, because that's what the chart says.

SINCERITY

What works for methodical and somewhat rigid parents will not work for those with a heart of butter. Look inside yourself sincerely and ask yourself what you are capable of. Be a rock for hours? Resist crying for more than a minute? And then ask yourself what you just can't stand. Getting up four times a night? Having an extra presence in the bed? Observe yourself and decide accordingly, without being a hero.

EVERY CHILD HAS A STORY

Take into account the character of the children. Just like us, some are calm and adaptable, others lively and rebellious. Don't make comparisons with other people's children. Perhaps looking at our child we see a little of ourselves and discover that he too, like us, takes a long time to fall asleep; the difference is that we read a book without disturbing those who sleep nearby, while he needs us and our attention.

OVER TIME EVERYTHING CHANGES

There are different stages in a child's life. Ask yourself if he has always had trouble sleeping. Was a baby brother just born? Have you moved home? Does the family argue a little too often? Is there tension? The disturbance of sleep is closely linked to what happens during the day in the sunlight and will go away after the baby has adapted. Maybe he just needs reassurance. In all cases, remember that time is on your side and that no 18-year-old is happy to sleep with mom and dad. You are not doing anything wrong. It's just a matter of resisting. Perhaps, even, to get over it.

GO-GO RITUALS

Trust the pre-sleep rituals, that is, the reassuring simplicity of the routine. Repeat the same actions every day, possibly in the same sequence. Always create the right atmosphere (no acrobatic wrestling before bed). The routine reassures and conveys the message that "everything is fine, everything is as always, you can sleep peacefully". Children grow fond of us: after dinner we play a little or watch a cartoon and then wash ourselves, put on our pajamas, dim the light. Mom or dad read a story, put the puppets to bed and go to sleep. Or at least, hopefully!

Only parents can know what is the best solution for their child, in the following pages we illustrate the ways suggested by pedagogists to deal with the thorny theme of bedtime but remember that only you can choose the most suitable.

BUT WITH THE SEVEN-DAY TECHNIQUE THAT WE PROPOSE YOU WILL BE ABLE TO OBTAIN GOOD RESULTS.

CHAPTER 1 The Sleep of The Newborn and The Child, From Birth to The First Years

Babies sleep a lot, because sleep is necessary for their development. It is therefore important to respect its rhythms and know its characteristics, also to help our children manage it independently and satisfactorily.

Thinking that a child's sleep is similar to that of an adult is very common but, at the same time, a wrong idea. In fact, sleep is a complex phenomenon that evolves and changes during growth. In the first months of life, we spend about 70-80% of the time sleeping: the hours of sleep for the newborn are about 15-20 hours a day, compared to five to six hours for the elderly person.

Newborn: sleep at 1 month of life

Many mothers worry because - they say - their newborn "sleeps too much". Let's start by saying that the newborn needs more sleep (always considering that each child is different from the other) and that then, as they grow up, this need gradually decreases. In this regard, numerous studies show that an adult need about eight hours of sleep a day, a fact which, however, is found only in adolescents and which decreases as age advances.

Babies and children in general sleep more mainly because sleep affects their growth, in particular by promoting brain development (especially sleep in the REM phase, ie the lightest one); consolidating the memory and everything the little one learns during the day; stimulating the secretion of growth hormone; strengthening the immune system; allowing the body to slow down and the brain to "cleanse itself" of toxins accumulated during wakefulness.

How long does a newborn sleep?

As already mentioned, about 15-20 hours of sleep per day are calculated for the newborn. Sleep also evolves throughout the day and is divided into cycles, lasting about an hour (90-120 minutes for older children and adults). Even during the night, the cycles follow one after the other; it is therefore wrong to think that sleep (of the newborn as well as of the adult) is continuous. Furthermore, within the single cycle (this also applies to both children and adults) there are “phases” that are different from each other in terms of amount of time. The 60 minutes that make up a baby's sleep cycle are divided between REM and non-REM. At birth, REM sleep represents about 50% of the total, at around 2-3 years it becomes 25%, to then reach (as in adults) about 20% at around 6 years. As anticipated, the percentage of REM sleep in children is higher because it is functional to brain development.

Micro-awakenings

We adults often wake up during the night between one sleep cycle and another. Often, we do not even notice it or we simply turn over to start a new cycle. The same thing happens to newborns and to the child in general, but more frequently (their cycles are shorter, therefore we speak of "micro-awakenings"), only that they are often not used to falling asleep on their own and therefore recall the adult to be supported: all this is absolutely normal, it depends on whether the little ones are frightened by the distance of the caregiver, a mechanism also present in the animal world and which constitutes a first defense of puppies from the aggression of predators.

In the event that the incidence of awakenings between one sleep cycle and the other increases, we speak of sleep regression, a phenomenon that occurs mostly in the following moments:

- Increased autonomy (when for example the child begins to crawl or walk) and spurts in psychomotor development,
- Separation anxiety, (around 18-24 months)
- First teeth,
- Entry to nursery or kindergarten,
- Arrival of little brothers or sisters,
- Mom's return to work,
- Family tensions,
- Change in family routines,
- Sleep disorders.

When we talk about "sleep disorders" we refer to conditions that generally occur in children aged 2 years and over, in particular the pavor nocturnus (night terrors), which appear after 2 years and can occur up to about 6 years, and most common nightmares. The first occur in the first hours of sleep and have a duration that varies from one to 15 minutes: the child appears agitated, frightened, can speak confusedly, cry, and all this can be accompanied by tachycardia, sweating, dilation of the pupils, increased muscle tone.

Nightmares, on the other hand, are notoriously associated with dreams with a frightening or distressing content and occur in the last hours of the night, in correspondence with sleep. While the content of the pavor nocturnus is not remembered, the nightmare is more easily recalled, perhaps precisely because it occurs in a lighter phase of sleep.

When is the newborn's sleep regularized?

In light of the above, we can understand how important it is to let the newborn sleep for as long as necessary, so that he learns to manage his own rhythms independently. In some circumstances, the baby can (or rather must) be awakened, for example if many hours pass between a feed and the other, but in any case, it is important that this happens possibly in the phases of light sleep, to avoid irritating him and making him nervous.

In general, the baby's sleep takes time to self-regulate. Many scholars have "idealized" models and studies relating to the different ways of managing and putting to bed that can favor this natural process. Let's see what can be done, from a practical point of view, to make bedtime easier not only for the little ones but also for us parents.

We accept that in the first months of life they can wake us up. As mentioned, this is neither a whim nor your management error.

We create an evening ritual that accompanies him to bed. Reading a story, singing a lullaby, in short, a routine or a set of activities that are repeated daily before going to sleep and which have the function of preparing him for what will happen soon.

We don't wait for him to be exhausted to put him to bed. A very tired child is more irritable and nervous and therefore more difficult to get to sleep. It is therefore preferable to avoid too turbulent or exciting games in the two hours preceding sleep.

Let's put him to bed where he will have to spend the night. Often children are made to fall asleep on the sofa or in the bed and then moved to their crib, and this can confuse them: waking up at night in a different place to where they fell asleep, they may feel scared and disoriented, and all this will make it more difficult to go back to sleep.

Let's observe him in everyday life and spend time with him. In this regard, any sleep difficulties and problems will give us a lot of information about the way he lives. We also consider that the more the child spends time with mom and dad during the day, the more he will be satisfied from this point of view and the less he will suffer from the "detachment" due to falling asleep.

Falling asleep also means separating from adults and facing something unknown alone: it is a learning that takes place gradually and is favored by the effective support of parents.

What are the main factors that help the child sleep peacefully in the different phases of psychomotor development? And what can we do?

Let's try to answer these questions starting from an awareness: sleep is a fundamental need and children try to satisfy it with the means at their disposal; the goal is to be in control of what will happen, thus being able to abandon safely and with pleasure to rest, both at the first falling asleep and after normal nocturnal awakenings or parasomnia.

The maturation of the states of wakefulness and sleep begins during pregnancy and is favored, in addition to genetic factors, by the health and psychophysical well-being of the mother. Disorders of pregnancy (such as growth retardation, gestosis, intense and prolonged stress) and childbirth (difficult births and various types of trauma) have a negative impact: children, even at birth, may have fragile waking and sleep states and immature, with long phases of agitation and a cry that is difficult to console; care, in this case, is more complex and many aids are needed to promote sleep: hold him in your arms, cradle, caress, sing lullabies, offer the breast ... These are precious aids, thanks to which the baby will calm down quicker and better, and will more easily develop the necessary self-confidence. Be guided by his requests and do not be afraid of establishing "bad habits" or "spoiling him": feeling listened to and understood by an adult who responds promptly to his needs (hunger, sleep, contact, consolation) is very important for proper development alternation between sleep and wakefulness, as well as good digestion and healthy growth.

Routine for falling asleep

Between 2 and 4 months the baby has a greater ability to adapt to the variations and rhythms of the environment (the alternation of light-dark, and social activities). This is a good time to propose activities that will be repeated regularly at certain times of the day (such as a bath or a walk), thus preparing for the arrival of 4 months, when the baby will suddenly become much more attracted (and distracted) by the external environment. He will begin to recognize and anticipate what is happening around him and will be ready to actively use the routines he already knows.

Predicting things that will happen, feeling that they depend on what he does and that his parents trust him and guide him helps the child develop confidence and allows him to manage anxiety about unknown and unpredictable events. It is now possible to reduce the child's dependence on the bedtime rituals managed only by the adult (who cradles him or takes him for a walk) and instead promote his active participation (through non-nutritive sucking, or curling up next to the parent).

At 4 months, infants who wake up at night in situations other than those in which they fell asleep - for example in a crib, when they were in an adult's lap or in another room - will have more difficulty getting back to sleep and will need help from parents to be able to go back to sleep the way they know. This is why it is useful to avoid changing the environment and sleeping conditions.

From this moment, and increasingly in the following months, the main help of parents will consist in strengthening the child's confidence in their abilities, helping him to discover, to experiment and to gradually do it alone, with adults as an example and guide.

The example of adults

At 6-7 months, when the maturation of the recognition of strangers and new environments makes it more difficult to adapt to novelty and to separate from the adult, the quality of sleep will depend above all on the emotional well-being of the child during the day. The predictability and active participation of the child in known routines, both day and night, will be of great help, while the inconstancy and unpredictability of the behavior of others will strengthen the child's "struggle" against the first falling asleep of the evening, make it less deep sleep (and therefore will wake up many times) and will contribute to a greater difficulty in falling back asleep and developing one's confidence.

Starting from this age, and even more between 9 and 24 months, the child counts a lot on you: he wants to learn the behaviors he sees in adults, and does so through imitation. He therefore needs examples to learn how to do it for himself according to the norms of our society. A parent who says to the child, "We are sleepy now," and accompanies him to bed by sleeping next to him, will have given him more effective help than an awake adult trying to "put him to sleep". As the child grows, we can decide together what to do before going to sleep: what to wear, which lullaby to sing, which book to read.

Night monsters

Around 3-4 years of age, the fear of the dark and of what could happen can manifest itself: at this age children live in a fantastic and imaginary world that they are not always able to control ("If you turn off the light, the monsters arrive!"). You can propose to look together for something that will protect him during his sleep and keep dangers away: a bracelet that gives superpowers, a puppet-guardian who keeps company in bed or a monster-chasing object to keep close.

Gradually the child's safety and sense of control will increase and, as they gain more independence, the child will begin to create their own personal rituals that will make them feel protected without having to involve other people.

Sometimes it takes a little pampering

Let's not forget that sleep problems, at any age, often tell us that the child is facing difficulties during the day. Pay attention to his new conquests and how he manages the most complex moments for him: separations, changes in routine or environment, new rules. He may need more closeness and listening to, to take a small "step back" before taking the next leap forward. In some stages of growth, children need more help than others: providing your child with the emotional nourishment that seems necessary will never mean "spoiling" him.

CHAPTER 2 Why Babies Don't Sleep

Does your baby have trouble falling asleep or does he wake up often at night? Here are the causes and the strategies to be put in place to improve the situation.

We know: children's sleep is the thorn in the side of many parents. One of the first questions you ask a new mother or a new father is: Does he sleep? In reality, children sleep, because sleep is a natural impulse and sleep is necessary to survive, only they do it differently from adults and therefore it may seem that they are not sleeping at all. In addition, there are various situations in which falling asleep becomes more tiring or give rise to more frequent nocturnal awakenings.

LET'S SEE WHAT SITUATION IT IS AND HOW TO REMEDY IT

1 It is still too small

It is absolutely normal for babies not to sleep continuously. Most children begin to sleep through the night between the ages of three and five. Of course: some even earlier, even when very young, but it is completely physiological that they wake up several times during the night's sleep.

This is especially true for the very young - up to two and three months of age - who never reach the deepest stages of sleep and for whom it is therefore easier to wake up.

Sometimes there are babies who sleep at night immediately after birth. On the other hand, most children succeed towards the end of the first year of life.

2 The environment is not suitable

3 The child is cold or, more likely, hot

4 He has nightmares

5 He suffers from separation anxiety

6 Nursery started

7 He is very tired

It may seem like a paradox but for many children it works just like this: the more tired they are, the more they struggle to sleep. It is useful to observe the baby's sleep cues - yawning, rubbing his eyes, staring at a distant point - to put him to bed just as they occur. If the moment passes, the child is in a state of hyper arousal which makes it more difficult to sleep.

8 Wakes up too late in the morning

If the baby never wants to go to sleep at night, one way to try to anticipate bedtime is to wake him earlier in the morning.

9 You have some health problems

All parents have experienced this: a common cold is enough to make the child sleep badly (and often the whole family as a result). The same also happens in the presence of other rather common conditions, including:

- cough
- atopic dermatitis (due to itching)
- sore ears
- asthma
- hypertrophy of the adenoids, which can lead to sleep apnea
- colic
- gastroesophageal reflux.

In these cases, we speak of secondary insomnia: sleep returns to normal as soon as the condition that caused the insomnia is cured.

Sleep is a particularly interesting topic and discussed among parents who like to confront each other, with an air very often resigned and tired, telling and sharing the physical and mental fatigue that the whole family suffers, if the child has problems related to sleep.

Sleep is a vital function of the human being: if you don't sleep, you die.

The quality of our days depends above all on the quality of our night's rest: this applies to adults, but also to children.

Depending on the age of the child, sleep needs are different.

Depending on the age of the child, parents are more or less willing to accept more or less frequent nocturnal interruptions; a mother with a newborn baby in her arms takes into account having to take care of the baby even at night, of continuous nocturnal awakenings at least in the first three months of life, where the baby regulates sleep-wake based on its physiological needs. Whether breastfed or bottle-fed, the baby wakes up numerous times at night:

the parents, however tiring it may be, willingly accept this situation, or sometimes try to survive it.

Starting from three months, the time between one feed and another lengthens: up to 6 months, the moment of weaning, in which the baby is expected to be able to sleep through the night.

It is emphasized that the times related to the development of the child are absolutely subjective and differ from child to child, from family to family: very often parents confront each other on these issues and come out disheartened.

"Other people's children are always sleeping more than our child and they don't have this problem ..."

Many parents complain of tiredness and exhaustion, disorientation and anger related to sleep problems that many children suffer from.

The reasons a baby does not sleep and does not meet parental expectations regarding sleep are:

- they do not know how to fall asleep by themselves: many children need the presence of the adult nearby, a hand, a caress, milk, a swing without which it is impossible to fall asleep. Good sleep education requires that the child after a ritual (a story, a song) is able to fall asleep by himself. This will allow him to sleep alone and in case he wakes up, to go back to sleep without being frightened; otherwise, he will look for the neighboring adult, the hand, the caress, the bottle or the swing, and if he does not find them next to him, he will be very frightened.
- children do not have a ritual but a transitional object with which to sleep: falling asleep time is a special moment, in which the child needs to be reassured by the

detachment that lives by the parents and the day and accompanied her to sleep with some ritual equal to himself who can calm him. Avoid overly lively games and exposure to TVs, tablets that excite rather than calm down. Reading a book, always the same one, reassures and calms; a quiet game, a song, a puzzle can be valid ways to accompany the child towards sleep.

If sleep problems persist, see a pediatrician to check for the possibility of organic problems.

WHAT TO DO?

Good sleep education is the first step

First, arm yourself with patience, love and willingness: encourage and support every success ... as well as every failure.

Furnish the child's room, making it comfortable and welcoming; children need their own space, clear and precise, circumscribed and defined. Different from that of the parents. If you do not have a room for the child, create a corner "of his own" with his cot and his toys.

Many children grew up in structurally small environments (in wartime few children had their own room), but if each had a space, a corner of his own, the boundaries were clear and were functional to everyone's growth.

From the age of 8 months, the child can manifest a fear of the dark: equip the bedroom with a small night light and perhaps organize, in case of continuous nocturnal awakenings, different lights that can allow the adult to move and run to the room of the child, without turning on the light. Light awakens and excites.

Do not welcome the baby in the double bed from birth: the big bed can welcome the moment of evening or morning cuddles, of play, of breastfeeding: not the moment of night sleep.

It creates confusion: there are no more boundaries and differences between adults and children this way. Children who get used to sleeping in their mum and dad's bed will always want to sleep in the big bed, because children are habitual and love predictability.

Create a ritual that the baby can enjoy and brighten the moment of going to bed. Read a book, sing a song; or make a drawing to hang on the bed that can keep the child company during the night who, when he wakes up, sees it again and feels reassured by it.

Offer the child a transitional object: a pacifier, a soft toy to fall asleep with, to cuddle in bed.

Many pediatricians already at birth propose the pacifier: if you do not share this opinion, you can opt for a teddy, a small soft toy.

In case of nocturnal awakenings, always go to the child, make sure that he is well (that he is not thirsty for example) and that he has not lost the pacifier, or the puppet, reassure him that "everything is ok", tuck in the blankets and go out.

In the face of tears and screams, keep calm, repeat all the gestures of reassurance and tranquility and proceed in this way;

maintain the right clarity. Children can be very insistent and provocative; if they have a goal, they put in place all the strategies they know, and they know they work, to get the result.

Proceed by trial and error: do not be discouraged, but arm yourself with strength and courage.

Being willing to change strategies by adopting different rituals and tricks depending on the moment, day and developmental period that the child is going through: what until yesterday worked today may no longer work.

Apply the slogan "give time to time": each child has his or her own rhythm, there is no need to be in a hurry or measure / compare evolutionary stages by making comparisons with friends and siblings.

Faced with structural or functional changes within the family of choice or of origin, the child can manifest psychological distress through insomnia, difficulty falling asleep, awakenings at night.

Events such as a move, a separation, an illness, the death of a loved one, work problems, the birth of a sibling can cause various psychological distress in children if not treated and dealt with adequately by parents.

In this case it is advisable to contact a psychotherapist.

All children, even those who have experienced some sleep-related discomfort, can re-learn to sleep well, alone and all night.

Among professionals today there is a tendency to talk about sleep education: be confident, everyone can do it ...

Correct, physiological sleep, especially in a child, is the result of a delicate balance between lifestyles, nutrition, habits, circadian rhythms (sleep is regulated by a biological rhythm, circadian, which regulates the states of wakefulness and sleep with a frequency of about 24 hours).

There can be many causes or circumstances that can lead to developing a sleep disorder in childhood.

Sleep disturbances are very common in childhood and cause discomfort and concern to parents.

It is estimated that about 25% of children may suffer from a sleep disorder during a time span from infancy to adolescence.

In most cases the problem "resolves itself" over time, but in some cases, it can persist causing emotional and behavioral disturbances.

Together with the baby, even mum and dad do not sleep well and this greatly affects the quality of family life.

When do we talk about insomnia in children?

A child suffers from insomnia when he delays falling asleep for more than 30-45 minutes, wakes up frequently at night without being able to fall back asleep quickly, or wakes up very early in the morning, at least much earlier than expected. If this happens for more than three nights a week, we can classify the disorder as infantile insomnia, the most common sleep disorder in children.

It is less common for the child to sleep poorly due to a pre-existing problem, for example sleep apnea due to obstructive problems of the upper airways (e.g., bulky tonsils), chronic diseases, pain. In these cases, we are witnessing the regression of the sleep disturbance, up to its complete disappearance, only following the therapeutic treatment of the triggering cause.

Often cases of infantile insomnia are the result of inadequate behavior of the parents at the time of putting the child to sleep, which concern methods, times and attitudes, and which lead to the establishment in the first six to nine months of life of a vicious circle that then self - maintains.

One of the most common sleep disorders in the early years of a child's life is called sleep initiation disorder due to the presence of association factors and nocturnal awakenings. These babies have developed the habit of falling asleep in certain circumstances, such as having mum and dad close, being held or cradled, drinking a bottle, hugging a soft toy etc. This involves the establishment of a sort of ritual in the child, who will identify the moment of sleep with that particular situation, and who in the absence of such circumstances, will not be able to autonomously resume the state of rest following a nocturnal awakening. This will require the recall of the parents, their constant presence or the need to recreate that particular circumstance to which the child has been accustomed.

Another typical sleep disorder is sleep difficulty insomnia associated with lack of rules and is typical of 2–3-year-olds, also known as inadequate boundary definition disorder. The child in question refuses to go to bed at the time set by mum and dad, if brought to bed he fights or cries, trying to get attention from the parents who could give in and thus delay the moment in which the baby will go to bed to sleep. This phenomenon occurs mainly in parents who are unable to establish and enforce firm rules for falling asleep.

More typical of 7-10 years of age, is insomnia from psychological causes and fears of falling asleep which is probably linked to a particular phase of psychological and emotional development. It is the age when children acquire the concept of death as an "irrevocable" moment. The problem can be triggered and perpetuated by traumatic events such as serious family problems, states of anxiety, stress. In this type of disorder, the child cries at bedtime and requires excessive reassurance, refuses to fall asleep; fears may partially or completely disappear if the child is allowed to sleep in the company of someone whose presence reassures him.

Finally, there is insomnia due to inadequate sleep hygiene, more frequent in the pre-adolescent and adolescent age group, in which bad habits begin to be established that negatively impact the quality of sleep and can cause a deficit of night rest and, in some cases, even daytime sleepiness. This disorder is mainly related to the use of caffeine-based drinks, the use of TV or video games in the late evening, daytime naps, or staying in bed longer than expected but not resting, which leads to a reduction of the night sleep load.

How can we intervene?

In light of what we have seen so far, it is important to remember that sleep is a primary need, in adults as well as children, and that bad habits or altered circadian rhythms can negatively affect the quality and quantity of sleep. It is also true that there is no single treatment that is suitable for every child suffering from infantile insomnia, but that the therapy must be personalized on a case-by-case basis.

On the other hand, parents will need to bring the sleep disorder to the attention of a pediatrician, especially if the child manifests unmotivated and persistent fears at bedtime, if he snores at night or has apnea fits, if he is very capricious or rebels continuously, if he is irritable or aggressive, or is very difficult to manage even in school.

If the child shows infantile insomnia attributable to poor sleep hygiene, a series of educational and behavioral approaches should be implemented to restore the child's circadian rhythms and eliminate any disturbing factors.

At any age of life, sleep hygiene is based on three fundamental areas of intervention:

The environment in which you prepare for sleep and sleep, which should be in the dark or in half-light, not too noisy and with a temperature suitable for the season;

Schedules, which parents should strive to keep as regular as possible and with daytime naps appropriate to the child's age;

The activities that take place before going to bed: it would be useful to establish a sequence of activities that accompany the child in the phase before sleep, such as eating at an appropriate time, taking a bath or a relaxing shower, listening to a story before going to bed, etc.

How to promote good sleep

Some things parents could do to help promote a good fall asleep and maintain peaceful sleep:

Establish regular sleep patterns (more or less regular times for falling asleep and awakening);

Create a positive ritual (bath, soft lighting, fairy tale and sleep);

Putting the sleepy but still awake baby to bed;

Leave the room before the baby falls asleep, so that he can acquire the ability to fall asleep on his own;

Prevent him from falling asleep while eating, drinking herbal teas, touching the parent's hair, while cradling him, etc. Otherwise, when he wakes up during the night to go back to sleep, he will need the same things to go back to sleep;

In the evening it is better to create dim light conditions and after 19:00 do not allow the child to use a PC, tablet, mobile phone to play;

The television should be turned off in the evening until the child goes to sleep;

To keep control of the situation in the evening, you must remain calm and speak to the child in a firm and decisive voice, showing him your affection, but also your firm intention to make him go to sleep at the set time.

If despite all the good will and efforts of mom and dad it is not possible to establish positive rituals and rules and the child sleeps very little, you can resort to the help of natural substances: passion flower, lemon balm, chamomile.

Used for millennia, these plants' ability to promote relaxation and sleep has been highlighted, even with scientific research. A balanced combination of titrated and standardized extracts of these plants can be of help to the child, limiting nocturnal awakenings and facilitating falling asleep. This can improve the quality of life of the child and parents and make the path towards good sleep hygiene rules easier.

The latest studies in this regard, in fact, have revealed worrying data regarding the long-term risks that children with sleep problems run, including obesity, low school performance, hyperactivity, but also high levels of anxiety and poor autonomy in school age and pre-adolescent.

This is why it is important to always remember that it is not necessarily just a question of "bad" habits; indeed, parents often wait so long to turn to a specialist that even if, initially, the crux could have been that, then inevitably other relational dynamics have been triggered that can make the intervention very difficult.

Among these, the dynamics of the couple must certainly be explored, because not infrequently the transition from the dyad to the triad presents difficulties that can influence (and be influenced) by a child's sleep problem. Another variable to be specifically investigated is the attachment relationship, which often, in order to be fully understood, requires deepening the childhood experiences of each parent and the relationships with their respective families of origin.

These are just some examples of the factors that could be involved in the problem, in reality it is neither possible nor useful to list them all, because each must be considered in relation to the specific situation, that is to the environmental and family context, but also to the individual variables that come into play. from time to time (e.g., the child's temperament, but also the expectations, fears and problems of each parent).

For this reason, it is really dangerous to simplify a sleep problem reported by a family, reducing it only to the incorrect habits that are detected: we risk "blaming" a couple of parents because they do not implement the right behaviors to make their child fall asleep, when instead, behind it there is a history and profound experiences that go far beyond the contingent situation and which are much more difficult to face.

Many parents often complain of the problem of children who do not sleep and in specialist practice this is highlighted as a widespread disorder in families with small children and beyond.

Cases of children sleeping with their parents until adolescence are not uncommon. Or rather, with one parent while the other retires to their child's bed, not just as an episodic reaction to stress but as an ingrained habit. This always emerges as a secret because the child does not want to be betrayed. This situation is often the icing on a cake of already serious difficulties.

Sleep difficulties are often accompanied by bad habits, left to grow and poorly managed by parents in the name of tiredness and fear of traumatizing their children, thus giving rise to problems that are really difficult to solve.

Sleep is an important physiological phenomenon of our life that occupies a large portion of time of the day, to a greater extent in the newborn, gradually less during growth and adulthood until it is reduced in old age to a shorter duration than in wakefulness.

Body and mind in sleep restore themselves from daily efforts and prepare for the new commitments of the day.

During the first year of life, the newborn (but also the fetus in the last months of intrauterine life) alternates phases of sleep and wakefulness of short duration, phases that group together and lead the child to a longer period of night sleep and some shorter periods of daytime sleep.

During the second and third years of life, daytime sleep is reduced to only the afternoon and from the age of four onwards it usually disappears.

Sleep and psychic development

The first year of life can be marked by sleep problems of the parents, more than of the children; it is they who often fail to adapt to the rhythms of adults. It is from the second year that the problems for the child can begin, because sleep is no longer a state in which one falls due to fatigue, but becomes like a different world from that of waking.

The child is just beginning to know the world and the transition between the two states is not so easy, he faces it at times with fears and anxieties, just like the transition from the familiar familiar world to the outside world populated with strangers and requires a certain maturity and a secure base to stay connected to and return to.

As in every phase of growth, the child must be accompanied to face the new experience and take it in. If premature or insufficiently managed, it can become a traumatic experience. Even the transition from wakefulness to sleep is presented with the same delicacy and parents must help the child to face the passage from the known and controlled world to venture into the unknown world.

For the first year of life, or at least for the first six months, children should sleep in the same room as their parents; this helps manage nighttime feedings and prevents SIDS (cot death syndrome). It is advisable to place the cradle or cot in the master bedroom, so that the child is always close to you.

Then it is good to cultivate the habit of sleeping that must begin during the day: it is good to stimulate the little ones with activities tailored to them: talking, singing and playing with them.

We must be careful not to over-excite the children, so as not to distance them from their certainties and their confirmations.

Then the most important step takes place: establishing a routine that accompanies the baby to sleep. You can take a bath, sing, listen to quiet music, read a story, cuddle. The child will slowly associate these activities with stillness and rest and will prepare himself for the nocturnal sleep. Babies need physical contact and often fall asleep in your arms. If they are relaxed and are about to fall asleep you can try placing them in the cradle or bed and standing next to them, letting them fall asleep.

It is not easy for the little ones to sleep in the cot, it is important that they feel the presence of their parents, even in turn, ready to cuddle and reassure them, to caress them and whisper words of encouragement; everything will be preceded by a decrease in activity, by tranquilizing separation rituals that bring you closer to going to bed: brush your teeth, put on your pajamas, tell the children a short story by being next to the child not in his bed.

Even the pacifier can be a valid ally: in addition to the relaxation it causes in children, together with the position on their stomach in the cradle, it counteracts the risk of SIDS.

Sometimes babies cry, move or fidget during the night. Although mothers tend to wake up at the slightest noise, it is not always necessary to get up to intervene; it is advisable to wait a few seconds, listen to what is happening and wait for the situation to calm down by itself.

Finally, if the child needs to eat or needs special care during the night, it is still good to remind him that it is night. To do this, it is advisable to speak softly, use soft lighting, make as little noise as possible.

CHAPTER 3 Sleep Training

Sleep training is the process of teaching a child how to fall asleep well by himself. By "well" we mean that your little one is able to sleep soundly for prolonged periods of time appropriate for his age.

For example: a 5-month-old baby can sleep for 5-8 hours continuously while an older baby can sleep for 10-12 hours.

Helping your little one fall asleep by latching him to the breast, rocking him or through any other technique is perfectly normal and natural. Most parents have used any technique to help their baby fall asleep at least once.

There's nothing bad! It can become a problem if your baby continues to wake up at night after five months and requires your continued assistance to get back to sleep.

The sleep training serves to teach to your baby to fall asleep by himself back to sleep alone if you wake up during the night. In order to sleep for longer and longer periods.

This is because you will have taught him how to relax and fall asleep on his own, instead of relying on your help.

The difficult aspect for many parents is to find a method that makes them feel comfortable and that is safe for their child. The sleep training often includes protests and cries from the children, and this, as you might expect, divides opinion.

Some moms and dads believe that sleep training is harmful to children, while others believe that it is selfish not to teach their children to fall asleep and deny them independent rest. It is easy to understand how the topic can be controversial to say the least.

It is right that you choose what is best for you and your family, but to do this you also need to have all the information.

Sleep training is the process through various methods is implemented by parents to help a child learn to fall asleep and stay asleep all night. It is started around 4-6 months

The three main approaches

Letting the baby cry (Ferber): typically, these methods suggest putting the baby to bed while he is still awake and allowing for short periods of crying alternating with the parent comforting the baby but not picking him up. Ferber states that in order to fall asleep alone and sleep through the night, babies must learn to calm down.

Tearless Approach: a more gradual approach - calming the baby in his sleep and quickly offering comfort when the baby cries

Fade Approach: parents gradually decrease their bedtime role by sitting next to the baby until he or she falls asleep and gradually moving the chair further away from the crib each night. Or even check your baby and reassure him (without picking him up) every five minutes until he falls asleep

Is sleep training risky or harmful?

Since it is possible for the child to complain or cry during the sleep training process, many parents wonder if it is risky or harmful. Or even if it can cause unnecessary stress and ruin the relationship between parents and child.

The short answer is that sleep training is perfectly safe when done following the correct path.

What does it mean? Sleep training does NOT mean leaving your little one in his crib and letting him cry for hours.

Sleep training methods should suit your little one's age, personality and family situation.

By following this logic, you will not cause any harm or stress to your little one and you will not damage your relationship. Indeed, it often improves it!

A rested parent has more energy and patience. Most of the moms I've worked with claim to be calmer and more present in the moment. It's easier to enjoy the little moments after a good night's sleep.

Unfortunately, some parents believe that the only possible sleep training method is to let their baby cry for very long periods (sometimes even hours).

I can assure you that there are several ways to teach your little one how to fall asleep alone and sleep through the night.

I have worked with parents who have chosen a method that allows them to physically comfort their little one and never let him cry for more than two minutes before picking him up and comforting him. Others have chosen to sit near their child's bed and cuddle him to help him fall asleep and gradually get him used to the bed.

When you have the opportunity to read well how these methods work it is difficult to define them as "bad" or "harmful".

Even if the parent leaves the room for a few minutes and then returns to comfort their baby, it would be an exaggeration to equate this method with abandonment.

You may need to push yourself slightly beyond your comfort zone, but I would never ask you to abandon your little one and let him cry for hours.

Research on the 'let it cry' method

Most parents associate sleep training with the Ferber method or also commonly called "let it cry". There are several myths associated with this method that unfortunately contribute to a negative association with sleep training in general.

The "study" on cortisol

Many of the prejudices towards this method stem from a study conducted 10 years ago by Wendy Middlemiss who studied (only) 25 children undergoing the "let it cry" method in a hospital.

The little ones were in no way helped to relax at bedtime and were instead placed in their cribs by the nurses with the aim of letting them fall asleep on their own. These babies were placed in their own cribs by people with whom they had no relationship without the presence of their parents.

Middlemiss analyzed cortisol levels in mothers and infants (on random days with no precise and rigorous detection on all study days) and concluded that cortisol levels in infants were consistently high indicating that this process was causing them unnecessary stress.

She further claimed that their levels were not aligned with those of their own mother.

The study carried out by Middlemiss has been heavily criticized over the years by other researchers and has also been discredited as there was a total lack of control, several errors in the data analysis and, of course, for the lack of data that were recorded selectively thus causing total unreliability of the results.

In essence, this is a roughly executed study that unfortunately caused many worries to parents who wanted to undertake a sleep training course with the best of intentions.

What the research on sleep training methods really says.

There are multiple high quality studies that show that sleep training is safe, does not cause any psycho-physical harm, does not affect the parent-child relationship in any way and has no negative long-term impact.

Importantly, most of these studies look at the "let it cry" method which is proven to be safe and effective. If you prefer to use a gentler, more gradual method, which usually involves even fewer protests and crying, you should have even fewer concerns about their safety.

As a parent I just want you to keep this in mind: there is a lot of false or incorrect information about sleep training. Do not let your loving home be compared to an orphanage or that a few nights spent teaching your little one how to sleep well can leave him feeling abandoned or psychophysically damaged. This is simply nonsense!

A well thought out sleep training program will not cause any harm and should only lead to a positive outcome for your family.

Another false myth is that sleep training equates to abandonment and that it teaches children resignation.

For example, the “let him cry” method is often associated with that used in orphanages in Romania in the 1980s.

Indeed, it was noted that such orphans never cried at bedtime (or very little). It was taken for granted that it was a symptom of their resignation as they had grown accustomed to never being consoled and comforted.

If you've ever done any Google searches on this, I'm sure you've even found results comparing these examples to what happens in a home with responsible parents who simply want to teach their little ones a new skill. In my opinion it is totally absurd!

I think I can say with total certainty that your little one's life is in no way like that of an orphan left on his own. So please don't let certain absurd associations make you feel guilty in any way.

In short: sleep training ...

- is proven safe in both the short and long term.
- does not affect the parent-child relationship.
- has a major impact on the mental health of the mother.
- is not the same as abandonment.
- can be done respecting your child's age and personality as well as your parenting style.

Does sleep training cause cortisol levels to spike?

Many parents worry about the stress hormone called cortisol and wonder if sleep training can cause a surge in this specific hormone.

The short answer is that there is indeed a slight increase.

However, it is important to keep in mind that, in both children and adults, it is normal to have slight increases in cortisol levels throughout the day. Not only is this normal but it is even considered healthy as it is a positive stress response.

According to Harvard University, there are three types of stress when it comes to children: positive, tolerable and toxic.

Does sleep training cause toxic stress?

Positive stress is what happens every day whenever there is a change in one's routine. At these times it is possible to observe a slight increase in the levels of this hormone along with a slight increase in heartbeats. It is a natural and healthy response that occurs when new situations are experienced and that helps the child to adapt to everyday challenges.

Tolerable stress is found in events of a much more impactful scope such as the loss of a loved one or a traumatic injury. In these cases, thanks to the presence of proper support, the child can learn to be resilient instead of being traumatized.

Toxic stress is caused by long-term abuse or neglect and is the only type of stress that can alter normal development, affect natural organ functions, and cause relationship problems between parent and child. This type of stress is what Romanian orphans were subjected to and it has nothing to do with your family situation.

Specifically, De Jong indicates how a child subjected to toxic stress often lives in family environments where parents very often yell or raise their hands (to each other or even to the child himself). Often there are also sexual abuse of the mother or child and the abuse of drugs or spirits.

So toxic stress is NOT caused by short-term changes made in a loving and responsible environment. Anyone who wants you to believe otherwise is simply misinformed.

Remember: toxic stress is the only form of stress that can cause permanent damage in children, including relationship problems.

Unless your little one grows up in a toxic environment like the one described above, you have no reason to worry that he or she will suffer harm of any kind. Especially when it comes to small changes to his routine such as those needed to do sleep training!

The positive stress response is considered useful for children to develop appropriate reactions and responses to daily events, and helps build resilience.

Your baby is growing up in a loving home, with loving parents. You can rest assured that by following a sleep training method you will not subject your baby to any toxic stress.

Will I have to listen to my little one cry during sleep training?

Since you are going to change his routines and habits, it is normal for your little one to protest. If he has always fallen asleep by latching on to your breast and all of a sudden you decide to teach him how to fall asleep alone in his crib, it is normal that he will go out of his way to let you know that he is not happy with this change.

He is unable to understand why this new routine is needed and, most likely, he does not like it. Crying can create anxiety in the parent forced to listen to it. I understand perfectly.

But keep in mind that a few days of protests (always supervised by you) can help your little one sleep peacefully through the night FOR YEARS. Many babies already cry normally at bedtime. In these cases, sleep training can actually help reduce the amount of crying.

It is good to remember that just because your little one is crying does not mean that you are doing him harm.

In a few years, your child will want to eat chocolate for lunch and you will obviously say no. Do you know how he will react? Crying out. He'll likely get hysterical even when you decide to turn off the TV while watching his favorite cartoon. I can assure you that one day she will even ask you to stay at home and not go to school and when you don't allow it you will see big tears flow down his face.

Being a parent is not all confetti. We have to make decisions every day to ensure a safe and healthy future for our children.

Learning to sleep well is probably as important as proper nutrition. While it is normal to expect a few tears when teaching your children to eat healthy foods, so it can be when teaching them to sleep well.

A well thought out and personalized sleep training program will not cause any harm to your baby.

The sleep training can and should be customized according to your family's needs.

There is lots of fake news on the subject that can inevitably cause stress and anxiety in a parent who is hypothesizing this path.

Mild and brief stress is a natural and healthy response to daily events. We are unable to prevent it. You are in no way harming your baby if you decide to teach him to fall asleep on his own if you use a non-improvised method (even if the method itself involves a small number of tears).

Toxic stress is the only one that can cause harm and it occurs only in certain and extreme circumstances. Sleep training does not come close in any way to situations of abuse especially if carried out in a safe manner.

IS SLEEP TRAINING REALLY NECESSARY?

It is a totally personal choice. Remember: never feel obligated to do something that doesn't make you feel comfortable.

If helping your little one fall asleep makes you happy, that's no problem. As long as your little one gets enough sleep for his age, is happy, develops properly, and sleeps safely, you don't have to change anything. Do not think that it is necessary to teach him to fall asleep on his own if the situation does not create any problems for you.

Just ask yourself if you and your little one are happy. See if you are both getting enough sleep. If you answered yes to both questions, you don't need to make any changes.

If, on the other hand, you feel exhausted and worn out by the situation, then you can consider using sleep training to improve the situation even in the long term. I mean YEARS of uninterrupted sleep, for your little one and also for you.

Another great benefit is that it could even improve your relationship. Research shows that when parents and children are rested, their union is stronger.

Finally, many parents become more confident when they see how happier and more active their children are as their sleep quality improves!

Breastfeeding and sleep training

What is the relationship between sleep training and breastfeeding? Some mothers are convinced that they must completely stop breastfeeding their baby in order to proceed with sleep training.

It is absolutely possible to continue breastfeeding your little one as long as you want and at the same time teach him to fall asleep on his own. Many babies still need at least one night meal (or two) until they are 6-9 months old. But are able to learn to fall asleep on their own as early as 5 months!

The important thing is to eliminate breastfeeding as a method used by our little one to fall asleep. It is possible to teach him to fall asleep on his own and then breastfeed him when he is actually hungry during the night.

Are you wondering if sleep training is the right path for YOU?

I realize that thinking of teaching your baby how to fall asleep alone may seem like too big a decision. If you decide to proceed, remember to follow a well-studied and not improvised method. Choose methods that can be easily adapted to your specific needs. And finally, never do something that doesn't make you feel comfortable.

Try to stay away from all those places where the goal is to make you feel guilty and judge your every choice. Unfortunately, there is much fake news on the subject!

When done correctly, sleep training can provide great relief to the family by restoring the joy of being together.

Of course, it's normal not to feel completely comfortable at the start of the journey. On the other hand, it is something new for you as much as it is for your little one. Sleeping well is a biological need. We need it in order to function normally and be happy with ourselves and with each other.

It is a feeling that every parent and every child should be able to experience.

Once the decision is made, you will realize that you have chosen the best for your family.

Remember that to start a sleep training path you need these 5 things:

1) RESPECT

It is important to respect the physiological need for sleep on the part of the child: pretending to incorporate it into an adult life and letting the little one accumulates too much fatigue or overstimulation, will make the process even more complicated.

We also respect the child's need for space. Depending on the various stages, he may need space to crawl or roll around the cot. And that's great! You have to let him do it and give him the opportunity to discover this completely new thing about falling asleep for himself.

Finally, there must be respect between the parents: both must agree and mutually support each other along the way.

2) COMMUNICATION

Think about what you are trying to say to your baby: "I know you are tired and irritated. I love you and respect your need for sleep. I'm here and I'll be calm and patient until you learn to fall asleep peacefully."

How do you communicate this message? Verbally, with shushing or songs; non-verbally with always consistent behavior and responses, and remaining calm and positive.

What is the child communicating to you? "Mom, I'm tired and confused, why don't you breastfeed or rock me as before?" The child is not in panic nor does he hate you. You are right there, using your touch, your voice and your warmth to pamper him.

3) CONSISTENCY

This is the main factor of sleep training. However, we see it, what we are doing is changing one of his habits and, therefore, his behavior. And to do this it is essential that messages always be consistent.

If not, we will confuse the baby and further extend the number of weeks it takes for results to arrive.

An inconsistent response, or even a negative reinforcement - such as letting him cry for 40 minutes and then attach him to the breast however, will ensure that the next time the child will show even more resistance.

So, remember: it is better to stop trying, take a break and try again after 1 hour. But don't reinforce the behavior you are trying to change.

4) PATIENCE

For gentle, crying-free sleep training, it can take up to 3-4 weeks before you begin to see your first steps. Not all babies respond within days! Everyone has their own times and, if we decide to stick to their pace, we shouldn't be in a hurry to progress.

Keep in mind that, along the way, there will still be many obstacles (leaps of growth, teething, vaccines, allergies, hot summer nights, entries to the nest or changing the baby sitter, etc.) And you have to accept with patience also days and nights of "no".

In any case, it is necessary to be absolutely dedicated and convinced of this path and have the necessary energy to carry it out even if it lasts much longer than expected.

5) CALM

Imagine what a state of mind a child is in who we are trying to make accept something new or different from the one he has always loved. Or a child struggling with the first few nights in the bedroom, away from parents.

The child will need all your calm and balance to be reassured that everything is okay. If you add your stress to his stress, it will spiral out of control!

You must be the anchor of this little boat in the midst of the waves and not let yourself be overwhelmed by the storm.

Babies have a special sensor to detect your anxiety, your fears and your sadness. Feeling these emotions at the time of falling asleep will not help the process at all, on the contrary, it will make it even more difficult for this to happen.

Bottom line: When you choose to work on your baby's sleep WITH the baby, you need to be confident, calm and happy that you have made the right decision for your family. Show your child that you know what you are doing and that this is best for all of you!

CHAPTER 4 The Ferber Method

The phase of nocturnal awakenings, is natural for children, but it is rather traumatic for the parents. Sleeping and restoring psycho-physical energies during the night are in fact essential phases to maintain the psycho-physical balance of each person throughout his life. When these moments are interrupted by the constant crying and moaning of your little ones, it is difficult to stay calm and go back to sleep. Therefore, it becomes essential to resort to the best tips to rest better, and the most effective remedies to prevent and manage the crying of the little ones. In this chapter we will talk specifically about a simple but appreciated method. It was developed by Dr. Richard Ferber, who drew up a series of rules for sleeping well, with particular reference to the sleep of the little ones. Take a few notes, test it personally if you see fit. Sleeping with the Ferber method could be the winning idea you were looking for.

Here's how to proceed After the goodnight kiss, leave the room. If the baby cries, come back after 30 seconds, calm him down, but do not lift him from the crib. Then go out again. If the baby starts crying again, wait five minutes before returning to him. Calm him down again (for no more than two to three minutes) and go out. Continue like this, increasing the amount of time you spend before returning to the baby by five minutes each time. The first day comes to 15 minutes. On the second day, start at 10 minutes and go to 20. Continue to take a 30-minute rhythm and keep it until the baby, after a few days, "gives up" and falls asleep quickly.

Extra Help

This method can be stressful, as many babies cry for a long time, which most parents struggle with. The best thing is to use a watch to know when to go back to the baby. But no kitchen alarm clock, so as not to disturb the little one who falls asleep. Stop re-entering the room as soon as you notice the baby is calmer, as your reappearance may trigger new screams of protest.

Possible cases

You need great firmness and there is a risk that you will give up too quickly. Alternate with your partner, taking it one day each. If you are a single parent, make sure you can count on the physical or telephone presence of someone who can give you the support you need: your mother, a friend or a neighbor.

CHAPTER 5 Letting Babies Cry Who Do Not Want to Sleep Is Not Dangerous

Are methods of making babies fall asleep dangerous for their development and do they affect the bond they form with their parents? Researchers respond through an experiment.

Let him cry; intervene; put him to sleep when he falls asleep; get him used to a time: these are just some of the advice that new mothers receive when trying to understand what is the best solution to make their child fall asleep without repercussions on his psyche once adult. But how should they behave according to psychologists? Are methods of making babies fall asleep dangerous for their development? A Flinders University study, titled "Behavioral Interventions for Infant Sleep Problems: A Randomized Controlled Trial", published in Pediatrics, attempts to answer and help parents and children find a solution to sleep problems.

The researchers compared two methods used to put babies to sleep. The first is called “graduated extinction” (or Ferber method), which asks parents, through several sessions of increasing duration, to let the child cry. In practice, the mother or father is asked to put the child in the cradle, go out and, in the event that the baby should cry, to return initially after 30 seconds, then after a couple of minutes and so on, so that the child learns to self-regulate. The second method, on the other hand, is called " bedtime fading", and involves the creation of a precise routine that "trains" the child to a certain regularity which, over time, allows him to fall asleep within the time set by his parents.

To understand the effects of these methods on babies, the researchers selected a group of 43 children between 6 and 16 months with sleep-related problems. Their parents, divided into two groups, were asked to follow the two methods described above and were compared with a control group. During the sessions of the experiment, each child was taken some saliva samples to monitor the stress levels in relation to the quantities of cortisol identified.

The data collected showed that the children on whom the parents used the “graduated extinction” method fell asleep 13 minutes earlier than the control group and woke less often during the night. The children on whom the " bedtime fading" method was used fell asleep 10 minutes earlier than the control group. As for cortisol, the scientists say they experienced an overall drop in levels for both methods compared to the control group.

The scientists' conclusions are that both methods tested not only help children regulate sleep, but have no long-term consequences on children's stress levels and on the relationship that is established with parents. In short, they would not be harmful.

CHAPTER 6 The Estivill Method

Raise your hand if you, among parents and in particular mothers, have never discussed the Estivill method: it is dangerous, it is not dangerous, it is effective, it is useless ... but there is no doubt that in the last twenty years this method of making children sleep has influenced millions of families around the world. Let's try to find out more.

In 1996, Dr. Eduard Estivill Sancho, a pediatrician from Barcelona, published the book 'Do la nanna' in which he describes an almost infallible method (valid, he says, in 96% of cases) to make children sleep who just do not want to know about falling asleep or who wake up often during the night. The Estivill method, which in turn refers to the system developed years earlier by the pediatrician Richard Ferber of Boston and published in the volume 'Solve Your Child's Sleep Problems", suggests, in a nutshell, putting the child to bed while still awake and educating him to fall asleep alone. The book is very successful (over three million copies sold worldwide), also because the system seems to work and many new parents tried by sleepless nights can finally breathe a sigh of relief. But at what price? In the following years, in fact, various associations of pediatricians mooted certain ideas about the Estivill method, denouncing its 'violence' and underlining that no scientific study has ever demonstrated its efficacy and safety. In 2012, Dr. Estivill himself partially retracted his controversial method of making babies fall asleep. But many continue to follow it ...

Estivil method: how it works and why it was successful.

How does the Estivill method work? The system devised by the Spanish doctor and illustrated in the bestseller 'Do la nanna' is based on the gradual extinction of crying. In practice, the technique is divided into three distinct phases:

- as an initial step Estivill recommends introducing a routine to be repeated every night before falling asleep (for example a warm bath, a small game or reading a fairy tale, to create a positive environment for him), then placing the baby in the cot and getting out of his bedroom (obviously the method assumes that the child has his own room, no co-sleeping with mum and dad);
- if, as is easily predictable, sooner or later the child begins to cry, one should not intervene immediately but let predetermined periods of time pass before running to him, gradually increasing them (initially 3 minutes, then 5, 10, 15, etc.);
- when you enter the baby's room, you have to comfort him without picking him up, until he falls asleep again. According to Estivill, this method produces excellent results against the nocturnal awakenings of children, even the smallest ones, in just one week.

Does the Estivill 'Go to sleep' method really work? Yes, the method all in all works, we don't know if it really works in 96% of cases and in just 7 days, as the Barcelona pediatrician promises, but it works. After all, it is natural: if the baby cries in his sleep but receives no response, after a certain period of time he stops crying and goes back to sleep alone. You just need to have the strength and patience to resist his cry, which in many cases can become downright desperate. Provided, however, that we know that crying is not a simple whim, but the only way that a small little creature (in Estivill's book the method is considered effective as early as 3 months ...). And that he stops crying alone not because he has regained his serenity, but because of exhaustion.

Is the Estivil method dangerous? The alarm cry of numerous associations of pediatricians.

"We now know from scientific research, if common sense were not enough, [...] that the claim that a small child falls asleep alone and sleeps through the night without requiring the presence and contact of the adult, as well as being anti-physiological and unrealistic, it can cause confusion in parents and great stress in children ". This is what the Cultural Association of Pediatricians thinks of the technique devised by the Spanish pediatrician. So is the Estivill method dangerous? According to its (many) detractors, this technique is devoid of any scientific evidence, because it is not supported by studies that have seen its effective application. It also does not take into account that every child is unique and different from birth, so we cannot think that there is a "method" for teaching how to fall asleep, or to overcome any nocturnal awakenings of the newborn, which is valid for everyone.

But, above all, a system that decisively represses the baby's crying, does not take into account, as already mentioned above, that with crying the baby expresses a need (which can be hunger, thirst, a malaise, etc.) or a state of mind or a simple request for reassurance. By not responding to his cry, the parents induce the child not to seek comfort when he is in a situation of discomfort ("no use crying, as mother does not come"), leading him to lose faith in the people who are closest to him. From a psychological point of view, it is essential that mum and dad are able to give him security, reassuring him and looking after him even at night (and patience for a few sleepless nights too many, love for your baby compensates for everything).

The Estivill method, from when?

The "right" age to start the correction of the Spanish pediatrician.

In the book "Fate la nanna" of 1996, about the age at which to initiate the child to the Estivill method, the pediatrician recommended starting very early with the techniques against the nocturnal awakenings of children (as mentioned, even from 3 months) given that "there is no difference between a newborn and a 4-year-old child." A very questionable statement that attracted the most ferocious criticism of him and one that he partially rectified many years later, in 2012, specifying that the rules of his method were valid only for children from 3 years of age who suffered from the so-called infantile insomnia due to incorrect habits: "Infants regulate their biological clock (which, however, is still immature at that age) on the basis of breastfeeding and for this reason it is absolutely inappropriate to force the rhythms of sleep and wakefulness. Better to start from the age of 3".

CHAPTER 7 The Tearless Approach

Just as Estivill / Ferber's 'tearjerking' method is criticized, so too the gentler methods are almost derided by those who believe that a few tears will do better than harm.

The sweetest methods are those that start from the premise of listening to your child, trying to communicate with him, taking care not to leave him alone in times of need. Crying is communication, listening to him and understanding him is essential for those who support less severe methods.

BUT WHAT ARE THESE METHODS?

Even with these methods it is important to establish a routine, everyone is free to choose the one they prefer or find most comfortable. Bath, pajamas, milk and sleep or have a massage, sing a lullaby. It is important to remember that every child has his own biological clock, a routine that follows these rhythms does nothing but better stabilize his schedules and thus making him fall asleep will be much easier.

On the other hand, if you linger too long in putting him to bed, the child risks getting excessively tired and then has difficulty falling asleep because he cannot relax, calm down.

SO, LET'S SEE HOW WE CAN RELAX OUR BABY

Among the things that promote relaxation are: fairy tales, a rocking chair that cradles him before going to sleep, a nice massage, a warm bath, a bottle of warm milk, a lullaby, pampering a lot, delicate and calm, minimize all external stimuli, avoid too exciting games, talk to him in a calm and low tone, a background 'white noise'; there are children who also relax listening to the sound of the hairdryer, or a fan or a dehumidifier. There are also devices for sale that simulate different sounds such as the waves of the sea, the heartbeat, the song of crickets, some even, disguised under stuffed animals, also simulate the noises that the baby listened to while he was inside the uterus.

All these ingredients, even mixed together, favor a relaxation of the child who will physically prepare to face the night.

Another good habit (this obviously also applies to those who decide to follow the Estivill / Ferber method) is to keep the room at a temperature not higher than 18 ° C and not lower than 17 ° C. Very often it is the temperatures of the room that determine the awakenings, therefore either due to heat or cold.

The gentle methods are divided according to the different techniques you prefer to use. In fact, precisely because they arise from listening to both the different characters of the parent and the child, they can have very different applications.

THE IMPORTANCE OF THE RITUAL

There are parents who drive the baby around in the car for hours, those who rock them, those who sing a lullaby, those who tell stories, I made my first child fall asleep by passing the lukewarm hair dryer over her body! Every parent finds the best way to calm her baby, and that's the beauty of it!!!

These are just small ideas, from which everyone can get an idea, if they consider it useful:

The sleep signals

- we have seen that the child sends precise signals when he is tired. We could give him "feedback" of what we have perceived using a "signal" of sleep, which could be a song, a story, or a simple word. For example: "Shhh, it's time to sleep", "Shhhhhh, good night". To ensure that these words are correctly associated with sleep, use them ONLY when the child experiences a pleasant situation, eg. when you see him almost asleep and calm? When the association has taken place then you can use them to help him calm down (the word or sound will "remember" the relative body sensation).

Prepare the "environment"

- it is unlikely that the child will have a signal that it is time to switch off if the lights are still on in the house, the TV going, the father working on the PC ... we learn the importance ourselves of the rite! We could turn off the lights and replace them with candles at least half an hour before going to bed, turn off all electrical appliances, go all together to the bathroom to wash, sing a sweet song over and over again, etc.

The bath

- a hot bath can be a good way to relax the baby before bedtime, better if done by candlelight and together with mom and dad.

The massage

- help our baby to perceive the sensations of his body, relax him, contain him, reassure him, what better way to prepare for a good night?

A favourite object

- personally, the "pet object" of my children has always been me and their dad, in fact they have always fallen asleep holding our hands or hugging us. We adults also like to share a bed with the people we love, I don't see why it should be any different for children. Having said that, I realized that in particular moments of life it is our own children who seek privacy, solitude, detachment. So, let's give it to him. We can help them detach themselves from us during sleep by using a "transition object" that makes them feel protected even without our presence. Many children use a soft, warm blanket, others a stuffed animal, others a doll, bring this "dear object" into the routine of falling asleep, giving it the importance, it deserves.

WHAT IF THE RITUAL NEEDS TO BE CHANGED?

Over time, a ritual that has always paid off could become obsolete, eg. I noticed that in an absolutely natural way the ritual I use with my children has changed from massage, to lullaby, to nursery rhyme, to invented story, up to ever longer and more elaborate stories. It seems obvious to me that we adults, always listening to the needs of the child, must make imperceptible but significant changes in the ritual, which thus assumes a RHYTHM (repetition of an event which, however, each time, alongside known elements brings new ones) For example, continuing to make a 3-year-old baby fall asleep in the same way as he did at 3 months implies keeping the baby tied to the past, to what is no longer. The child remains "small" internally because he is not allowed to look for other ways, to make the effort to change, to grow. Trying to protect him too much is actually doing him a disservice.

Now, one of the strongest and most difficult associations to change is the suck-sleep association. The association between sucking (breast, bottle or pacifier) and sleep is the most natural, sweet and pleasant that the baby can have. Sucking is "magical" and allows small children to calm down, fall asleep, as well as be fed, of course. The problems that can arise are:

- As I said earlier, the child is not allowed to try other avenues.

- It is difficult for a mother to tolerate the situation for several hours of the night for years (perhaps precisely because it is not as "natural" as it is believed: nature provides for women to have a birth every 18/24 months, if you observe puppies of animals you will notice that when the mother is ready for a new pregnancy, she removes her puppies from the breast, sometimes even violently, but this does not cause them any "trauma": they had everything they needed.)

- The bottle syndrome (if a sweetener is present in the bottle liquid, formulated milk, juice, tea, herbal tea, this could cause tooth decay. A less frequent but not non-existent syndrome in breastfed babies).

- The bottle or the breast as a comfort to fall asleep can lead the baby to feed beyond his real needs.

Now, how can this natural association weaken over time, which the child will hardly be able to change without our intervention?

The Pantley-Style

Gentle Removal method: choose a "good" night where you notice sleep cues and your baby is fine. To make the baby fall asleep, or to make him go back to sleep when he wakes up, do as you are used to (with bottle, pacifier or breast), but instead of leaving him like this and falling back to sleep, as soon as you notice that the need has been satisfied and the baby is half asleep, gently remove the nipple (or pacifier or bottle). Especially in the beginning, the baby will start looking for them, but if you can, touch them gently under the chin or on the lips to help them close their mouth. you can also use the "sleep signal". If the baby seems not to calm down then offer him breast again etc. until he looks almost asleep again then proceed again. It can take up to 5 attempts, but generally beyond this limit the child will fall asleep (otherwise it means that it is not the right time, or because he has some discomfort, or is too nervous, etc. then wait for a more auspicious day). Use this method only in the evening and at night until the association between sucking and sleeping becomes less strong. Generally, it will be the child himself who, as soon as he is satisfied, will detach himself and turn to the other side to sleep. At this point it will be natural for him to seek less and less external support to sleep and consequently the afternoon nap and night sleep will improve, without even a shed tear or tiring back and forth.

Keep a "diary": while trying the methods described above you can keep an account of the nights, to verify that the situation is actually improving and to monitor the needs of the child, eg. if in any case and with every method the child wakes up at 3 in the morning it means that his is a real need and therefore it is right to be patient and wait for events to take their course.

All the methods described above are not against breastfeeding, on the contrary, the fact of learning to listen to the baby, to recognize his real needs, to offer him valid alternatives, allows mothers who wish to continue breastfeeding for a long time to fully enjoy moments of intimacy with their children, knowing that this is the real need and not an act due to "habit". I believe that in this sense breastfeeding then fully carries out its duty, not because it is the only choice, but because it is ONE, personal and conscious choice.

Day / Night

The first step is to learn to distinguish between day and night. The newborn sleeps without distinction both day and night, distributing sleep over 6/7 intervals and this is necessary for it to feed properly. But right away, begin to make him tell day from night, so it is important that daytime naps are in a lighted room, with daily noises of the house, and in a different place from the room of the night. At night, however, we make the house darker and more silent. Generally, already around the year the child regulates sleep to 2 daytime naps (usually mid-morning and mid-afternoon) and around 2 years (but even earlier, for some) to nap (also quite long 2/3 hours) in the afternoon. Of course, it all depends on the type of child we have; however, we try to make the child perceive the difference between day and night.

Sleep Noises / Need to be breastfed

During sleep you will notice that the baby moves and makes noises. Not all the movements and noises the newborn makes mean "I want to latch onto the breast". So, we learn, before offering the breast, to "listen": we wait for his signal, we wait. The little one may fall back asleep on their own just by hearing your breath. If he wants to be breastfed it will be easy to understand!

We are listening.

Listening to the baby does not mean, in my opinion, giving him the breast every time he cries, but learning and observing his signals. The child tells us that he has to evacuate (read Living without diapers) that he is hungry, that he is tired, that he is bored, that he is sad and that he is sleepy, etc. It is not said that for every eventuality the breast is indispensable! A mother who listens knows how to give differentiated answers according to the needs of the child. A child is not able to detach himself from the world on his own and understand that he needs sleep (as an adult can do) so it is up to us to tune into his signals to accompany him in self-discovery. With regard to signs of fatigue, it is very important to respond quickly, because a child put to sleep when he is not tired will get nervous, a child kept awake beyond his means will no longer be able to fall asleep easily and will have restless sleep.

Do you need breasts to fall asleep?

Yes, if we want it! That is: is it good for a mother to offer her breasts to sleep up to 5 years of age? Very well, everyone chooses for himself! But let's not confuse what has become the routine for the child with his actual need! A baby who has been offered no other alternative but to sleep on the breast will not be able to freely choose what is best for him, he has no choice! For the child, rhythm and ritual are fundamental, but this does not mean that the ritual cannot be gradually changed with the advancing age and with the change in the needs of the family. If you feel that offering the breast to your baby is no longer ideal for you then let's learn how to create a new ritual of falling asleep.

- ✓ shared sleep
- ✓ the gentle method of habituating the child to gradually fall asleep without external media (pacifier, breast, bottle, etc.). Proceed so: by the breast (or bottle or pacifier or rocked or whatever) if he cries, to calm him down, then when he seems calm but not quite asleep, pull it off. This is so the child finds by himself, slowly and gradually, the ability to fall asleep without external support. If he cries, give it back to him and proceed again. Go on like this until the baby stops correlating sleep with having the breast (or other) as a pacifier and learns to fall asleep alone. It is always useful in these cases to find a new "ritual" of falling asleep (at 7 the lights and voices are turned down, everything is turned off, we wash ourselves, put on our pajamas, a story, a lullaby, etc. or a bath at 7, at 7.30 drying and massage, pajamas, lullaby, etc.)

Also keep in mind that the age ranging from 8 to 12 months sees a first glimmer of awareness arise in the baby, who consequently has more fears to face. The second "crisis" of the age ' is between 2 and 3 1/2 years, when it begins the age of NO.

Having said that it is important for the baby that the mother is well and feels confident in what she is doing, so don't listen too much to "methods" recommended by others, but do what you feel is right for you and your baby.

CHAPTER 8 The Approach of The Fade

A fussy child makes you hectic parents. Inevitably, the parents will be next to the baby until he is sound asleep. As for how to put the baby to sleep, a lot can be done so that parents can be free from fidgeting over babies near bedtime.

Yes, sleep time for demanding babies can be trained by doing certain methods.

One method of putting the baby to sleep can be used with the fade method or moving away gradually.

What is the fade method?

In the fade method, parents gradually reduce their role in accompanying the baby to sleep by sitting next to the baby until he falls asleep, and slowly move away at night. The other approach to the fade method is to check on the baby and clma him (without lifting him) every five minutes until he falls asleep.

How to do the fade method?

To do this, put the baby in a crib or bed, pat his back or body parts until the baby feels comfortable. Position yourself a little out of the baby's reach, you can be near the door or on the edge of the bed and start leaving the room slowly. Check the baby every 5 minutes, you can go back briefly to check if the baby's condition or position is fussy or not.

Some experts say it's okay to nudge the baby until the baby feels comfortable. While other opinions suggest talking softly and kindly to the baby and saying this is his bedtime. Do this regularly and consistently. Create a goal where within two weeks you should be able to leave the room after saying "good night". And you don't have to pet or silence the fussy baby until they fall asleep.

The purpose of the fade method

This is a way to teach children to know their bedtime well. The method of moving away gradually is so that the child is used to sleep without having to have a parent figure accompanying him during sleep. This method is also known as the method where parents slowly disappear from a child's perspective, or parents can sleep outside the child's room.

This method takes a time, it doesn't work right away. So parents need to be patient with the conditions and intentions of sleep training for this baby.

Another goal is to give the child time to find ways to calm down. "Suppose you are the coach, not his hold on sleep," said Kim West, social worker and author of 'The Good Night of Sleep, Sleep Well', who fights with the strategic fading method. This method can be done for kids aged 5 months and preschoolers.

Which fade method is effective?

A long-term study found that infant sleep methods are applied through better fading methods. The impact of depression on their parents is also less. Each child has a character and so the method is applied differently, so not all children can be successful with this fading method.

Your role as a parent is very important in applying and adapting sleep patterns and healthy daily routines for each child. Adapted to your needs and age.

CHAPTER 9 How to Deal with Separation Anxiety

Around 6-7 months, babies experience separation anxiety away from mom. In this phase of growth, in fact, the child begins the process of individuation: that is, the child begins to feel like something psychologically separate from the mother figure, hitherto experienced by the child as one with himself (the so-called symbiotic phase). It is a phase that has nothing pathological or abnormal about it; indeed, it is normal, useful and necessary for the correct psychological development of the child. And in fact, at this age the child begins to explore the world around him and begins to open up to the outside. But he is also afraid, precisely because, if until then he was one with his mother, now he is "alone" (or so he thinks he is ...), struggling with something that seems so interesting, but also disturbing.

The fear of abandonment

This identification inevitably generates the fear of being abandoned by the mother and this fear manifests itself (even in the child until then quiet and who, all in all, respected a certain daytime-nocturnal sleep-wake rhythm) typically when falling asleep, when the child, although sleepy, he seems to refuse to fall asleep, or during sleep, with frequent awakenings, even partial, accompanied by crying.

Why? Because, in the specific case of sleep, for the baby closing his eyes is equivalent to not seeing his mother any more and, not seeing her, for him the mother is no longer there. He has not yet "understood" that even if he does not see his mother, she is still there and has not abandoned him, that the reassuring voice of his mother from his room means that his mother will "come", that the very presence of his father (in this apparently useless phase, since the baby generally only wants his mother and calms down only with her!) is reassuring because there is still someone able to take care of him while waiting for his mother to arrive.

It is obviously a very complex experience, and not as linear and conscious as described.

What can be done?

It is difficult to answer this question, not so much because this phase is difficult to solve. Sooner or later the child, if substantially calm, will overcome it. It is not possible to give directions because every family context is unique: every couple of parents must find their own way to accompany the child in this delicate moment of growth.

The starting point is to reassure yourself that it is something normal, not pathological, that all children go through. Indeed, it is a necessary phase, which must be accompanied, not blocked. The child must be reassured by two adult parents, who in the face of the child's panic do not get anxious themselves, becoming hysterical (because there is no reason!). Or, vice versa, by "compassion"(For what? It is not a serious problem; it is indeed a useful phase for growth!).

There are no magic solutions. However, here are some tips

Better to have the baby sleep in a bed (or at least put him down still in a half-sleep) than in your arms.

When the child wakes up and starts crying in his bed, it is better to hold on and keep going back and forth from his room (even the father, because in his own way he must be involved in the management of the baby, even if his action seems little effective) rather than taking the baby into your bed.

To precede one's arrival in the room by attempts (initially completely useless, or so it seems) with the voice, perhaps reassuring the child that "you are coming". It is better for the father to intervene first and then, at a later time, for the mother. Do not attach it to the breast or do not offer the bottle immediately and in any case not always. Basically, it is necessary to look for a gradual and progressive intervention that helps the child to understand that this (the voice of the mother who reassures him) is followed by this other (the appearance of an adult), until even the first step can be enough for him to calm down.

Keep the lights dim, however, and avoid playing with him. The message that must pass, even with the expression of the face, is that "at night we sleep": not hysterical anger but a firm and, as far as possible, calm attitude that transmits the reality of the moment (that is nothing tragic, but even pleasant).

During the day, playing hide-and-seek (hiding your face for a moment with your hands and then returning to show it): slowly teach the child that even if something is not seen that something is the same, and it will reappear (including mom!).

Measures such as giving milk or herbal teas during awakenings should be avoided, because they risk creating habits that end up maintaining awakenings over time, rather than attenuating them. Nor is it useful to try to distract the child by playing with him or taking him to the living room, perhaps by turning on the television: as we have said, the child must clearly receive the message that "the night is for sleeping, not for playing". In the case of a father who reported during the 3-year-old check-up that he had finally solved his child's sleep problem, even if to make him go back to sleep he had to go up and down with him every night, in the lift about thirty times ...

The preparations to promote the baby's sleep, usually with a vegetable composition (lemon balm, passion flower, chamomile, valerian), give modest results; some results are sometimes obtained with melatonin, administered in the evening, before sleep, and continuously for a period of at least 15 days to evaluate its effectiveness. If so, evaluate the opportunity with your pediatrician (strictly avoiding do-it-yourself), without excessive hopes and without excessive feelings of guilt.

One last thing: don't think there are “magic” solutions. The path remains slow, gradual. It is necessary to give a child (and any person) the time to gradually overcome their fears, their doubts. Expecting from him, as from yourself, to find the solution overnight means losing sight of the development of a child and the dynamics of people who are, instead, slow and gradual.

CHAPTER 10 The Montessori Method

GETTING BABIES TO SLEEP CAN BE A VERY STRESSFUL TIME IN THE LIFE OF THE NEW FAMILY.

Let's talk about Grazia Honegger Fresco, the last living disciple of Maria Montessori, who dedicated herself to spreading and divulging this theory.

The pedagogist Grazia Honegger Fresco, a pupil of Maria Montessori, in her book "Let's go to sleep" gives parents valuable advice to get the little ones used to sleep.

The pedagogist advises to follow the baby's rhythm and slowly accustom him to sleep at night and stay awake during the day. The baby's circadian rhythm depends a lot on the time he was born. If he was born in the morning, he will sleep during the day and will need more time to get used to the night's rest.

Manage your baby's sleep with Montessori tips.

Leave the child free to play, try, experience and live his little "adventures" and emotions. It is good to let him free to acquire his skills (turn on his side, crawl, small sensory experiences as he grows) without forcing him into high chairs or bouncers.

However, the reverse is also not good: the child should not be overstimulated.

Do not use the pacifier excessively: as soon as the baby cries it is good to console and reassure him by making him feel his presence. If the pacifier becomes self-consolation, we will not be able to understand the reason for the crying (that is, the only tool that the baby has to communicate with us) and will look for it at night in the same way he looks for it during the day.

Make him move during the day, no bouncer, high chair or baby seat.

The child has to move and consume energy during the day. He must have a busy and interesting day to sleep well.

A baby during the day must be left on a rather large surface so that it can learn to move on its own side or to crawl ... While constricting objects block his development.

They are comfortable means for the adult but do not respond to the natural motor evolution of the child. A child forced during the day by these improper means becomes stressed and his malaise easily results in restless sleep.

Let him play alone

Maria Montessori used to say: “Care is the adult's task; play is the work of children”. This means that the adult must not interfere in the games of the little ones, because it impoverishes them, replacing them with different mental mechanisms that make the child passive.

“If the adult continuously acts as a protagonist in play situations, the child does not experience at his own level the experience of free choice of his own actions, of creating in his own way. And this has a negative impact on daily physiological needs, as well as on his mental abilities". Play, exploration, testing himself, are all activities that contribute to making a child independent and an independent child will be able to manage his sleep and wake rhythms well. In fact, if he spends time playing on his own during the day, it will be easier for him to be alone in silence at night.

Don't give him the pacifier as soon as he cries.

The cry of a small child is high pitched and is predisposed by nature to make parents intervene. But don't get upset or run with a pacifier to calm him down. Just make him feel that Mom and Dad are there. Caress him, calm him down with a hug. Don't give in to the urge to stop crying right away. You have to learn to tolerate his wailing and understand what he really needs.

Offering a pacifier immediately, even to prevent crying, means giving a unique response to a malaise that an adult is unable to interpret.

"With the pacifier always ready, sucking becomes the predominant self-consolation and this fixes the baby on a very limited and repetitive oral pleasure that goes on over the years with also negative effects on language" explains the pedagogist.

The pacifier makes life easier for parents, but it is not an advantage for the little ones.

Another bad practice is teaching him to suck his finger. If a child does not do it spontaneously, there is no need to anticipate behavior that is not necessary.

To make him listen, be kind but decisive.

The child needs a safe track on which to proceed. If a parent always says yes to every request, the child will feel more powerful than the parent and this feeling frightens and angers.

Another thing that makes the child fragile is to put him in front of continuous choices. Asking a child: "Do you want to go to bed?" it means giving an image of an insecure parent which makes the child insecure in turn. The parent's task is to decide for the child's good. But many are afraid of oppositional reactions or of running into tantrums. How do you make sure you are heard?

The solution is to speak to the little one in a gentle but decisive way. Having polite but firm ways, with no alternative choices, gives the child peace. If at the time of going to sleep, one calmly says "Now is the time to go to sleep", the child perceives that it is the inevitability of the things that must be done daily and this transmits tranquility. Read also: How to be obeyed by children without shouting (and why it is better).

If he wakes up with a bad dream in the morning, tell him that you too have had a nightmare.

If the little one shouts after a bad dream it is better not to turn on the light, but simply to be close to him, in silence, caressing him and making him feel your hands on his body ...

In the morning you can tell yourself that you had a bad dream that scared you. The child must indirectly find himself in this story, without anyone alluding to what he experienced. In this way the little one feels that what he has experienced also happens to others, even to his parents.

What to do in the evening.

Create a ritual, which is always the same and through which the child understands that it is bedtime. The advice is to avoid television and too lively games after dinner.

Communicate to the little one in a sweet but decisive way that it is time to go to sleep.

Bath, dinner, pajamas and book are an excellent ritual even for when the little one grows up.

To monitor their sleep, many experts recommend keeping the baby in our room until the age of one year.

It is important to go to him if he calls us at night, to calm him down and avoid separation anxiety, increasing his trust in us.

Reassure him in case of bad dreams, without turning on the light but with physical presence and an adequate tone of voice.

CHAPTER 11 Naps

Baby naps are a very valuable ally for their growth, but how do you get your baby to nap? Precious tips to help you rest and create a routine.

How to get your baby to nap

The naps of newborns are essential for correct and healthy growth and also for the psychophysical well-being of parents, who can take the opportunity to rest, be together, take care of personal chores or simply catch their breath.

We know that routine is extremely important for the serenity of the child, who immediately needs reference points and help, also to distinguish between day and night, between night and day sleep.

For the first three months of life, the newborn spends most of his day sleeping, and slowly his biological clock will stabilize also thanks to the routine that will be proposed: feeding, bathing, sleeping. Then as the weeks go by, the daily naps will become more distinct and the waking moments will be clear and enriched with games and interaction with the mother. There are usually three naps during the day: one in the morning around 9.30, one around noon and one in the afternoon.

Here's everything you need to know about naps.

The early morning nap is important for the growth of the baby, the sleep is heavy and can last up to two or three hours. Experts advise not to encourage a nap before eight in the morning, even if the child woke up at dawn, in order not to delay the times of the whole day.

At around six months, the baby may abandon the early morning nap, and settle on two naps a day, one around noon and one in the afternoon.

It should last at least 45 minutes.

To facilitate the nap, you can recreate a "mini sleep routine", as you do in the evening for a night's sleep: a little fairy tale, a cozy atmosphere and a lot of tranquility.

Never put your child in a position to skip a nap, perhaps hoping that he will fall asleep earlier in the evening. The nap, on the contrary, promotes sleep and reassures the child, its lack has only the effect of further irritating him.

Turn off the television when it's nap time because it has an exciting effect, turn off the cell phone and unplug the phone and politely explain to those who want to visit you that this is not the right time.

No to active games, to somersaults with dad, to songs before a nap.

Don't feel guilty if you choose to go out and have your baby sleep in the stroller. There is nothing wrong with that, maybe you have to accompany your little brother to school or you have a commitment. Between the afternoon nap and night sleep should not pass more than 4 hours, otherwise the child becomes nervous.

Around 15 months, the morning nap disappears and you can't force a baby to sleep if he doesn't want to.

Around 3-4 years, even the afternoon nap is abandoned. Often this change coincides with the start of kindergarten with its extended hours, but it depends on the children and the days. You also need to consider how tired the baby is, in which case it is worth trying to keep him awake, anticipating the meal and putting him to bed earlier than usual to make him sleep through the night.

When even the afternoon nap has disappeared, the child will be ready to live a non-stop day awake and collapse exhausted around 7.30 pm. He will sleep about 12 hours a night.

CHAPTER 12 Naps: What to Know for Each Stage of Growth

How many naps do you need and how long should they last? Here's how everything changes from year to year.

Every new parent knows the pains (and joys!) of making babies sleep through the night. But afternoon naps are also key: they affect the quality of their night sleep as well as their mood throughout the day. Here's what to do for each stage of growth.

Infants (0 to 3 months)

What to expect: at first, sleep is a completely relative activity: babies don't sleep at set times and there isn't much difference between day and night. (According to the American Academy of Pediatrics, infants typically rest around 16-17 hours per day.)

However, between 8 and 12 weeks of age, it is finally possible to see a sleep cycle, which sees the child gradually get used to staying awake during the day and sleeping at predefined times during the night. So says Jodi A. Mindell, Ph.D., Author of Sleeping Through the Night, associate director of the Pediatric Sleep Council of Philadelphia. "Once you enter this phase, you will probably find that the baby begins to feel sleepy after being awake for about 1 1/2 hours or 2," explains Dr. Mindell. Don't worry if you don't notice a more stable rhythm until around 4 months - some babies need a little more time.

How to educate to sleep: try to catch the signals that your baby gives you when he begins to be tired: irritability, redness around the eyes, lost gaze or the instinct to touch the ear. Of course, you can try to make your baby fall asleep. "Maintaining daily habits will help convey the message to the child that it is time to let go in Morpheus' arms," says Dr. Mindell. You can, for example, lower the blinds, read a book, sing a lullaby, speak in a calm voice or whatever is required by your nocturnal habits.

From 4 to 12 months

What to expect: after the first three months, the baby's sleep begins to follow a more predictable pattern. Between 4 and 8 months, infants' sleep is usually clocked at specific times of the day, or is distributed into shorter, more frequent naps after a period of about two hours of activity, says Dr. Mindell. From 9 months on, almost all babies sleep at set times.

How long do naps usually last at this stage? From 4 to 6 months, it is generally 3-4 hours divided into three naps, which in the 6-12 month range become 2-3, concentrated in one or two sessions. So reports Jennifer Waldburger, social health worker, co-author of The Sleepeasy Solution and co-founder of Sleepy Planet Parenting. "When between 6 and 9 months, babies enter the phase that leads them to abandon the third nap, it is possible to notice that this often becomes shorter: it is what I call a" light nap", which can last as little as 20 or 30 minutes," says Waldburger.

How to educate to sleep: repeat the routine gestures that precede a nap with ten or fifteen minutes of preparation for sleep, Waldburger advises. Put your child down when he is relaxed, but before he is exhausted. "When babies get too tired, their body produces a stress hormone called cortisol - this substance makes it harder for them to calm down and can cause sleep cycle disruptions," says Waldburger.

The ideal time is when the baby is sleepy but still awake. "Letting the baby calm down on his own without rocking or nursing him until he falls asleep means that if he goes into a light sleep phase during the nap, he will know how to calm down on his own," says Waldburger.

Children from 2 to 3 years

What to Expect: "Most 2- to 3-year-olds limit themselves to just one extended afternoon nap, usually after lunch," explains Dr. Mindell. It usually lasts between 90 minutes and 3 hours.

How to educate to sleep: "In the transition from two to a single nap, two tendencies can be seen: either the second goes on long enough to affect the child's ability to rest peacefully at night, or the child simply refuses to sleep the second time, "says Waldburger. That will be the moment when you will understand that it is time to get rid of the second nap.

"During this transition phase, it is ideal for bedtime to take place in the middle of the day," says Waldburger. The time from 11:30 to 12:00 is the most common to start. "If your baby is still in the habit of having his morning nap, gradually postpone it by 15-

20 minutes every two or three days until you get to a start time around 11:30 am," suggests Waldburger.

Preschool age (4 to 5 years)

What to expect: While many children give up their nap appointment by the age of four, others continue with this habit until they are five: the time slot they usually doze in is between 12 and 13:30 (going on average to bed at 8 pm). However, even if your child no longer naps, it does not mean that you need to eliminate rest time altogether. "As your little one grows, the so-called 'nap time' can be replaced by quiet time," says Dr. Mindell. "This space guarantees everyone the opportunity to carve out a moment of peace during the day, while encouraging a nap in case of need."

How to educate about sleep: It's often easy to tell when babies are finally done with naps. "You will find that your little one no longer falls asleep during the times he used to do, or that if he skips a nap, he is still fine and shows no signs of letting up," explains Dr. Mindell.

CHAPTER 13 SLEEP TRAINING IN 7 DAYS

THIS METHOD CANNOT BE USED UNTIL AFTER THREE MONTHS.

You have survived the first three months, got to know your baby and understand his sleep cycles.

Now is the time to find some rest.

Before starting with this method, make sure that the child is in a positive phase. If he's getting his teeth, it's not the best time.

Day 1

Start a regular routine.

Children tend to confuse day with night. This happens because parents tend to blur the environment during daily naps. The child must understand the difference between nighttime and daytime sleep.

Always wake your baby at the same time in the morning.

On the first day, wake your baby up at the time you got him used to waking up and place him in a crib by the window. If the baby falls asleep for his nap do not dim the lights. Leave the shutters up, if he wakes up with the light of day the child begins to understand that it is time to wake up. This helps him to regulate the circadian cycle. Similarly, if the child wakes up at night and it's all dark, he understands that it's time to sleep.

In the evening, choose a time to put him to sleep, which is respectful of his tiredness. Remember a too tired child is short-tempered and falls asleep with more difficulty.

Give him a bath, put him in pajamas. Get close to him sing a lullaby, read a story, do something that indicates a new phase of the day separate from the others.

Give him a massage, but not tickle, the baby needs to calm down and not get excited.

Day 2

Practice Makes Perfect

Stabilize the routine. If your baby still needs to feed at night, do it in very low light - try to keep a relaxed atmosphere and not excite the baby. It must be a very soft transition from sleeping to waking up to going back to sleep. It is night, it is dark, there is no noise.

Conversely make daytime feedings most stimulating. Touch the baby's foot, sing a song, stand in bright environments. It is day, there is light, the little one will begin to understand the differences.

Try to understand what calms the baby in the evening. Each child is different from the others. If your son after bathing is as lively as ever, maybe you should eliminate this as a bedtime ritual.

Day 3

THE CRYING BEGINS

Put him in the crib when he is tired but still awake. It gives him time to calm down before falling asleep.

Make sure he has his own room or space with white noise or music. Or a soft toy.

Even if he falls asleep in your arms make sure he's awake when you put him in the crib.

The baby will start to cry but as we have seen, this cannot harm his development.

I know it's hard to hear your baby cry, but maybe that's just because you've changed his routine.

Maybe finding a toy in the crib will distract him and he'llstop crying. Or with the hair dryer on, or low music he'll stop soon. Look for something that distracts him but without your direct intervention.

Remember that it may be easier to use this technique with a younger child than with an older one. 5/6-month-old babies have their own routines and little "vices." Their resilience may be greater and they may cry more. Babies under 5 months usually cry for a maximum of 15 to 20 minutes.

I know twenty minutes will hurt, but the aim is to have better nights for everyone. Hold on.

This is your first fight of nerves with your son. Don't give in!!!

Check your baby often and reassure him with your voice, but don't pick him up for any reason. Don't give him the pacifier. Remember if exhausted from screaming after 10 minutes, you walk up and take the child in your arms, he will learn that you just have to cry uncontrollably and the next time will be even harder.

You will see that he will eventually calm down.

Day 4

Difficult

You feel guilty. Your baby cried, you challenged each other, know that today will be better. In the evening, repeat the same ritual, the baby will start crying again, but he will stop earlier and cry less intensely, because he knows that he did not get any results the previous evening. So don't frustrate your efforts and don't pick him up at the first hint of tears. You will see that the torment will end earlier this evening.

Day 5

Towards Stability

Usually with this system already on the fifth day most children find their own state of tranquility. If your child is very stubborn and still crying, extend your attention to 15 minutes.

Also evaluate the reaction of your baby, if when he sees you he increases the tone of the cry to be picked up, perhaps it is better that you observe him from a distance.

Some scholars say children need frequent parental reassurance, others consider it a mockery and this increases their frustration.

Try to understand your child's reaction.

Controlling the baby is more effective in calming your guilt than is for him.

Manage nighttime feedings and nappy changes in night mode in silence and in the dark.

However, try to reduce nighttime feedings. Remember that with proper nutrition, if your child eats less at night, nothing happens. Often, especially in older children, night feeding is a pampering habit, to spend time with you. But you have all day to play and stay together. We sleep at night. And also remember that the more food you give him at night the more he needs diaper changes, another reason to interrupt sleep.

Day 6

The Baby Sleeps Through the Night.

You did it, you put the baby in the crib when awake, he made a slight cry and then fell asleep. But you are not yet convinced of it, go back and forth between the bedroom and your bed, will he sleep? Will he sleep well?

Everything is going well, maybe now it's your turn to relax and accept the detachment. Your child is growing up, becoming less dependent on you.

How do you feel? Go back to bed and reflect on the fate that your child is already growing up.

Day 7

Everyone In the Family Sleeps.

Congratulations, your child sleeps in the bedroom and you can sleep, talk, laugh with your partner without fear of waking your child.

Enjoy your privacy even if just for sleeping.

Of course, most of the work is done, you will have more sleepless nights when your child gets sick, or a little brother arrives, or you are on the road and he is afraid to sleep alone.

Remember to manage your daily rest well with naps, to make your baby sleep better at night.

CHAPTER 14 Tips for Sleeping: The 10 Rules of A Good Night

This period of health emergency, which saw the closure of schools, work activities and various businesses, caused a disruption of the circadian rhythm of sleep for everyone, both adults and children. The absence of a routine punctuated by school, physical exercise and running up and down for appointments between snacks in the park and the pajama party at the friend's next door, affect the quality of sleep and therefore our biological clock that warns us when it's time to go to bed.

This is why, never before, it is important to carefully observe the rules of sleep hygiene.

1. Respect bedtime every night

A good habit to transmit to your little one is to establish and maintain a time to go to sleep, so as to adjust all the other times at home and, therefore, the rhythms of the family accordingly.

2. Make him always sleep in his room

It is good for your little one to follow a bedtime routine that sees him in his crib. It is wrong to make him fall asleep on the sofa while watching television, but accompany him to the room when the time has come, perhaps with a soft light, and in the background a sweet lullaby for children.

3. Separate the feeding phase from the falling asleep phase

The third point calls attention especially to new mothers, as it concerns the little ones. In the very first months of life, you cannot know when he is going to fall asleep, but in the following months you can pay attention to some signs, such as sucking with less force or the eyes that are no longer able to stay open, which warn you that you can detach him from the breast and place him in his cradle.

4. Respect meal times

Try to keep the same lunch, snack and dinner times regardless of what day it is, thus adjusting your times to those of your little one.

5. No to electronic devices after dinner!

Press OFF on any type of device you have at home: the child must not play or stay with the tablet or any other type of electronic device before going to bed, as their light interferes in the production of melatonin, causing difficulty in falling asleep.

6. Don't give him too much water or snacks before bed

Also, in case he wakes up during the night, it is advisable to avoid trying to reconcile him to sleep again by drinking warm milk or other liquids such as chamomile. Experts advise, instead, to help the little one go back to sleep with a comforting object or the so-called Linus blanket.

7. Beware of light!

When we talk about circadian rhythm, we refer to our biological clock that regulates the sleep-wake rhythm marked by the alternation of light and dark. Don't turn off the lights during the afternoon nap;

- ✓ at night, reduce light sources as much as possible;
- ✓ facilitate awakening with natural light.

8. No to stimulants after 4pm!

No to:

- ✓ tea, if desired, only decaffeinated;
- ✓ drinks containing caffeine;
- ✓ chocolate;
- ✓ sweets - candies - doughnuts – chocolate.

9. Favor a balanced diet

Let your child discover the goodness of foods containing fiber and prefer foods rich in tryptophan. The latter is a precursor of melatonin, and you can find it in white meats, blue fish, green vegetables, legumes and cereals.

10. Everyone in his own bed!

After the baby is 10 months old, it is good to get him used to autonomy and to let him sleep alone in his own room. In case he wakes up, go to him, comfort him and make him go back to sleep but leave him in his bed.

Try to follow these rules that will be useful for both you and your little one.

CHAPTER 15 Co-Sleeping: What It Is, Pros and Cons

Co-sleeping means letting babies sleep in the same room as their parents, close to their mother, in a cradle attached to the bed or even in the bed.

THE SPREAD OF CO- SLEEPING. Co-sleeping is a practice that has been gaining more and more ground in recent years and marks a turnaround with respect to the widespread thinking among mothers and pediatricians until some time ago. In the wake of the success of the theories that re-evaluate the importance of a "return to nature" in the mother-child relationship, such as breastfeeding on demand instead of timed breastfeeding, bonding, etc., even co -sleeping is spreading more. But let's see what it is.

Co-sleeping means the practice of letting the newborn sleep next to the mother. So, in the first place we refer to the parents' choice to put the child in bed with them or in a cot very close to the bed. Until a few years ago, this practice was considered by many as a "sign of weakness" on the part of the mother. Parents had to get the little ones used to being in their own bedroom right away, on pain of loss of privacy and the risk of not being able to send them away from the bedroom later on.

ADVANTAGES OF CO- SLEEPING. In recent years, however, there has been a re-evaluation of the importance of sleeping together. Both from a psychological point of view, since babies really need to be close to their mother, to feel protected and pampered; and from the point of view of organization and night rest for the mother. Especially in the early days, with very frequent breastfeeding, having the baby next to you is certainly much more comfortable than always having to go to another room.

NEGATIVE SIDES OF CO- SLEEPING. Certainly, co-sleeping reduces if not eliminates the privacy of the parents, but other solutions, times or places in the home can certainly be found where the couple can rediscover the intimacy lost at night. On the other hand, a concrete risk, for many doctors, is linked to the SIDS danger, or the terrible event of cot death. SIDS is linked to respiratory problems and sleeping in the same bed with the newborn, for many specialists, could increase the risk of this tragic fatality. The solution, however, comes from the manufacturers of childcare and articles for children: without having to mention any brands, there are now several brands that have studied excellent solutions to be able to practice co-sleeping avoiding keeping the child in the bed. These are cradles with only three sides and special extensions to be " hooked " to the parents' bed, so as to constitute a normal continuation of the mother and father's mattress. In this way the little one can sleep next to the mother in complete safety.

CHAPTER 16 How to Help Babies Sleep Alone

It often happens that there are boys and girls who struggle to sleep alone in their cot. Often these are transitory situations, but it also happens that these become real difficulties. Often the boy or girl needs to fall asleep with mum, or wants to sleep in mum and dad's bed. What could be a situation of cuddling and tenderness (having your child come to play in the bed with mom and dad) can become a real problem when one of the two parents is forced to sleep on the sofa, or in the bedroom of their own little son. In the couple this can generate strong tensions and even misunderstandings, often the father tends to accuse the mother of excessive care, while the mother defends herself by telling the father that he is insensitive to the problems of the child. Whatever the case may be, the child who cannot sleep alone often generates a conflict between the parents and is the signal that something is wrong.

So how can you help your children sleep alone?

First of all, it is necessary to differentiate children who absolutely do not want to fall asleep without the presence of at least one of the parents, from situations in which the child can have frequent nocturnal awakenings which then involve mom or dad having to help the child get back to sleep.

It is necessary to ask ourselves “what is our child afraid of?”

This question is crucial, because whether the child does not want to fall asleep alone, or whether he is no longer able to fall asleep alone, behind this difficulty “there is always a fear”. It is good that the parents first of all talk to each other about this problem and try to "get their own idea"; in their opinion what is the fear that does not allow their child to fall asleep? Once the parents have dealt with this, they can then choose which of them "feels safe enough" to talk about it with the child. Basically, there is nothing exceptional to do, but simply share with him / her that they (the parents) think he / she may have some fear that will not allow him / her to fall asleep. Talking with children doesn't have to be "an interrogation" and it doesn't have to be "you have to do this!" It means understanding through the words of your child what scares him, what does not allow him to detach himself from you to slip into the world of dreams!

Parents must talk to each other, especially to understand if there is something in family or social life that "can affect" and interfere with the safety of the child. Know that behind great fears, there are great insecurities, and that not falling asleep alone means making up for these insecurities, it means not doing it alone. As babies learn to walk alone, to eat alone, they also learn to sleep alone, this is part of the normal psycho-physiological development of the child.

Children who absolutely do not want to sleep alone are often the most problematic children, for them it must be understood that it is "impossible" to separate and detach from mom or dad. In this sense, as is done with the pacifier, or as is done with the diaper, it is necessary to find a mediator, who acts as a bridge between being with mom and dad and accepting not to be there anymore. The mediator, who can read fairy tales, listen to relaxing music, hold his hand until he is asleep, is not important in himself, but it must be understood that the mediator cannot be a technique. There can be no technique that replaces the need for "understanding" of mum and dad. This is why I believe that the key to solving the problem lies in the dialogue between the parents, and of the parents with the child; the 'how to' can emerge only through mutual exchange. All the more reason these considerations are also valid for nocturnal awakenings, often fewer problematic situations because the child has already learned to fall asleep by himself!

Often the search for techniques (in my opinion) is an attempt to find a shortcut to what could instead become the couple's difficulty in dealing with a problem that can become truly relevant. The dialogue between parents is the salt of the "couple relationship" but also the center of family life; when this dialogue cracks or dries up, then it can happen that the whole family system is affected (including the sleep of children). Techniques (which can be useful indicators) cannot replace your understanding! Coming out of the logic of easy blame, it is essential to know that children (on a psychological level) feed on the understanding and words of their parents. This is important to know, because it is on this that the responsibility of being parents revolves!

To learn more about what parents can do for their children, I would start from the idea of being able to distinguish whether the problem of children's sleep may be something that is already present in the first months of life, or if it has arisen suddenly and unexpected in a later period. Grasping this distinction allows us to understand if an adaptation of the child has occurred in the delicate transition from "intrauterine" to "extrauterine" life, or if the child has managed to acquire the fundamental rhythms of his own development (such as food and sleep) or if, on the other hand, this passage has not occurred completely and somehow some of these rhythms find it difficult to establish themselves in a harmonious way with respect to the style and family habits of the parents.

A couple who find themselves having a child who has problems sleeping alone should take some time for themselves, in which to be able to talk calmly and without haste (suspending the daily pressures of family life) about these topics. What really matters is that each of the two parents develop their own idea on the subject ... often what I find in my practice as a psychologist is that of meeting parents (who for various reasons) are unable to develop their own point of authentic view to believe in. The importance of having a credible point of view is to generate motivation and orientation in the things that need to be done; what matters is not so much the immediate result, but the beginning (also by trial and error) to trace a path that means changing the way of doing or communicating in the couple, and the couple with their children. Often it is these changes (which we can consider as the landing of a new understanding) that allow for the resolution of sleep problems.

CHAPTER 17 Does Your Child Not Want to Sleep? Try One Of These 25 Strategies

1 - Avoid looking him in the eye

The last thing you want before your baby goes to sleep? Him getting too excited and agitated. Did you know that looking him in the eye for a long time is really stimulating for him? And for your baby it means: "Ok, it's time to play!"

So, pay attention to eye contact when trying to put him to bed or try to calm him down if he wakes up in the night. The same goes for his favorite song or his play of the heart: at night, if he wakes up, avoid all this.

2 - The Baby Bath

Warm water and loving massages are a real relaxing cure-all. And the same goes for the little ones too. Forget noisy games, however, keep a low tone of voice and be relaxed while bathing your baby.

3 - Co-sleeping

For or against co-sleeping? Several studies show that babies who sleep this way with their parents grow up more confident and less anxious. But be careful: better in safety, with the cot next to the bed. (The American Academy of Pediatrics does not recommend sharing the same bed with the child.)

4 - Sweet dreams thanks to the last feeding

Is your baby one of those babies who wakes up hungry at night? Then you could give him the last feed before bed, even if he is still asleep. There are those who believe that this way their tummy will be full enough to gain some extra sleep for you and for him.

5 - Cot? No toys

The cradle? Only with your baby: everything else is more dangerous for the baby and can cause suffocation. All that is needed on the mattress is a blanket or sleeping bag.

6 - The right fragrance

Some scents can lull your little one to sleep. For example, lavender, placed as an essential oil on a handkerchief in a small bag near the bed, can help to relax him. However, fragrances are not recommended for babies under six months. And also, for those with too sensitive skin or nose.

7 - Beware of reflux

It is a common problem in babies with sleep problems and is caused by a malfunction of the cardia, a valve between the esophagus and stomach. Seeing your pediatrician can help you figure out if there is really reflux.

8 - Help yourself with your hands

Try to gently place your hands on his tummy, arms and head when he is in the crib. Comfort and pamper him. Sometimes your closeness may be enough for him to feel safer and fall asleep.

9 - Pay attention to the right time

Put him to bed when he's tired.

10 - Natural fiber pajamas

How sweet are those pajamas in the shape of a frog? But be careful: it is better to avoid synthetic fibers and say yes to natural ones, such as cotton. They are less irritating to the skin.

11 - Temperature

It's nice to fall asleep with the right room temperature, right? It's the same for your baby too. The American Academy of Pediatrics, to prevent SIDS, recommends a room temperature between 18 and 21 degrees Celsius.

12 - Lights? Better a dark room

Put him in a dark room. Forget night lights and use heavy curtains if the window frames don't block the light enough.

13 - How beautiful are massages!

Do you know that babies who have been gently massaged for about fifteen minutes fall asleep earlier than those who have only listened to one story? A study by the University of Miami Touch Research Institute says so. Let's try it right? Massage gently.

14 - The importance of the nap

It is important for you, as it leaves you the space to rest, shower or check your cell phone, but also for your baby. Napping helps your little one's mind grow and develop. Don't skip your nap just because you're afraid he won't sleep all night.

15 - The diaper at night

It can be boring to have a wet diaper at night. Change it only if it wakes up or has pooped.

16 - Pacifier

It can rock the baby until bedtime and several studies show that it can also protect against SIDS. However, it should be introduced after the first month of life and naturally (without immersing it in sweeteners). If your baby rejects it, don't force it, and if he loses it, don't put it back.

17 - Do-it-yourself remedies

You never know what may or may not work. There are children who fall asleep cradled in toy swings, dads who drive around the block to make the child collapse or who turn on various appliances to create the so-called "white noises" that so relax the children. No one is here to judge: if you find your remedy, and it works, keep using it. The important thing is that it is safe for you and for the baby.

18 - How beautiful is routine!

Babies like routine and it helps them understand that it's time to go to sleep. Choose a ritual before sleep and keep repeating it.

19 - Bedtime story

It doesn't matter which children's fairy tale you are telling: it is still relaxing for your little one and they love hearing you tell a story in a calm, relaxed voice. It is a good habit to carry on even in childhood.

20 - Anticipate the signals

Anticipate your little one's signs of fatigue instead of waiting for him to fall asleep. He may rub his eyes or yawn. Many too tired children have a hard time falling asleep, reacting to the opposite and thus confusing their parents.

21 - The importance of the voice

Do you know your baby recognizes your voice? From birth it is something familiar and that has a positive effect on him. Talking to him in a calm and calm voice can help the little one slip calmly into Morpheus' arms knowing that he has his mother by his side.

22 - white noises

Do not leave him in absolute silence. In the womb your little one was used to always hearing sounds, such as your heartbeat or your stomach. Some babies fall asleep more easily with white noise, such as a fan or any household appliance.

23 - Cuddles, cuddles, cuddles

Here's one more excuse to pamper him. There are never enough! If you smother him with hugs and kisses before going to bed, he will feel even more loved and secure. And you will ensure a more peaceful and prolonged sleep.

24 - A little music

From Brahms to Beyoncé - your choice doesn't matter. Music and singing are perfect ways to calm your baby down. Singing helps lower your stress level, so it's good for you too!

25 - Sleep

Zzzzz .... What is this sound? It's your baby who fell asleep. Now stop talking and enjoy the silence ...

CONCLUSIONS

IN ORDER TO GROW UP PEACEFULLY, CHILDREN NEED TO FEEL THAT MUM AND DAD LISTEN TO THEIR NEEDS.

There is an emotional synchrony that allows the child to trust adults, recognizing them as those who help him grow. To become autonomous and independent, in order to experience new behaviors, they must feel loved, they need warmth, attention and trust: only in this way will they be able to experience that separation is only partly frightening.

This need to be understood and listened to and reassured is greater during the night, when darkness and silence can be a source of anxiety and fear. When the baby is asleep, he needs to feel safe and for this to happen he must continually experience that the people who care for him are always available.

Remember that the reasons why your child is not resting well may be physical, psychological or inadequate sleep strategies. To this is added the personality of the little one.

It is therefore always important to identify the set of reasons that can cause restless sleep and evaluate their importance.

If you can't solve your baby's sleep difficulties with the tools you find here, seek expert help.

As we have already seen, sleep is divided into cycles (it is therefore wrong to think that sleep is continuous) and each cycle has the duration of:

- ✓ 50 - 60 minutes for infants
- ✓ 90-120 minutes for older children and adults.

The 60 minutes that make up a baby's sleep cycle are divided into 2 phases:

At birth, REM sleep represents about 50% of the total, from 3-6 months it begins to decrease, reaching 25% towards the year. Around age 6 (as in adults) it is about 20% of total sleep.

1) REM phase or " active" sleep. What happens to your child?

During REM sleep, our brain is active and dreams appear, breathing and heart rate are irregular. Sleep can appear agitated, the child can open and close his eyes, complain, move and this is the time when it is easier for him to wake up because his nervous system is not yet mature and is ineffective in blocking the signals that depart from the brain in the direction of the muscles. Furthermore, the little one has not yet developed a system that protects him from external noises and internal sensations, so it is very likely that, at this stage, he can wake up.

PS Observe your child, you may think that he is awake but in reality, he is continuing to sleep, he is in REM phase!

2) Non-REM phase or "deep" sleep.

The NRem phase is divided into 4 sub-phases, from 1 to 4, depending on the depth of sleep (4 is the deepest sleep).

Up to 3-4 months of life, the deep sleep of newborns has only phases 1 and 2, phases 3 and 4 are not present, for this reason it is really difficult for a baby to sleep soundly before four months!

During deep sleep states, blood supply to muscles increases, energy is restored, and hormones responsible for growth and development are released.

In the transition from one sleep cycle to the next, children can wake up and ask for help from mom and dad to get back to sleep.

Parents can encourage and support their children to develop new strategies for falling back asleep on their own from 6-7 months of age.

Sleep is very important for growth, in particular, it:

- ✓ Promotes brain development (in REM phase, neural pathways are built which will later lead to language development);
- ✓ Consolidates the memory and everything the little one learns during the day;
- ✓ Stimulates the secretion of growth hormone;
- ✓ Strengthens the immune system;
- ✓ Allows the body to slow down and the brain to "cleanse itself" of toxins accumulated during wakefulness.

The sleep of the newborn (0-3 months)

Newborns sleep from 10.5 to 18 hours a day in an irregular way with periods ranging from one to three hours, both day and night, they often wake up as they need to be fed, changed and above all reassured and protected. Your baby, who until recently was safe and warm in your tummy, needs to feel close to you, otherwise he gets scared and cries. With crying, he draws the attention and care of mom and dad, only in this way is survival guaranteed.

Thanks to these treatments, which we will call proximal, the mother helps the baby to regulate his vital parameters, such as breathing, body temperature, the production of stress hormones. The child activates the proximal cures, waking up and calling back the mother, day and night!!!!!

Furthermore, inside the uterus, the baby is lulled by the maternal movements and the water in which it is immersed softens every blow. Whenever the baby moves, he has a chance to find and feel a boundary and therefore never experiences emptiness around him. As the months go by, this place becomes more and more tailor-made, thus giving the creature the opportunity to feel embraced in every part of its body.

When a baby is just born, he does not fully perceive his own body, in the sense that he does not feel where it begins and where it ends. Only through contact with adults can he feel that he is a delimited unity. That's why babies fall asleep and sleep better if they are in contact (while if we put them in the crib they cry), they need to feel physical boundaries, they need containment!

So, when you pick up your child, sleep with him, carry him in a swaddle, respond quickly to his cry, you are not spoiling him, you are responding to a fundamental need: to feel safe and at the same time allow him to develop trust in you.

The child experiences the need for closeness and contact both day and night and it is precisely during the night, when the house is immersed in silence, without noises or stimuli capable of reassuring him, that the child will feel the fear of loneliness and abandonment.

Co sleeping (sharing a room while sleeping) can be a good answer to the baby's need for closeness

Among parents and experts there are those who support and those who reject this choice. Opinions are mixed and mothers and fathers often find themselves torn in choosing "the best solution".

Personally, I believe it is important to listen and share the needs of the couple, communicate, observe your child and choose how to respond to his needs. I do not think there are solutions suitable for everyone, I do not think there are unique rules as well as for the rest of the questions: choice of times, sharing or not, meals, what to eat, who to attend, which kindergarten to choose etc. If you do not feel that choice is yours, you will not be able to make your baby feel good.

Whichever choice you make, remember to ensure your baby sleeps safely!

Co-sleeping and bed sharing

Sleeping together essentially means sleeping in close proximity to the baby. It could be in the same bed or just in the same room. Some solutions adopted by families:

Sidecar arrangement: firmly attach the crib on one side of the parents' bed, next to the mother. Three sides of the crib are closed, but the side next to the parents' bed is lowered or removed so that mother and baby have easy access to each other.

Different beds in the same room: have the cot close at hand or simply in the same room; prepare a mattress or cot for the older child on the floor next to or at the foot of the parents' bed.

Benefits of shared sleep

Sleeping together isn't the best solution for every family, but it can have many benefits:

- ✓ Parents often sleep more;
- ✓ The baby fidgets and almost wakes up when he needs to be fed, but since he is right next to the mom, the mom can breastfeed before fully waking up;
- ✓ Breastfeeding at night is easier when the baby is close;
- ✓ Breastfeeding overnight helps maintain milk supply;
- ✓ Sleeping in the same room as the baby reduces the risk of SIDS by 50%;
- ✓ No nighttime separation anxiety;
- ✓ Less trouble falling asleep;
- ✓ It's nice to wake up next to a smiling baby!

Creates a safe sleeping area for your baby.

Any surface your child uses for sleeping (including baby beds, nap surfaces, or adult beds) must be safe:

The baby should be placed on his back to sleep.

The sleeping surface should be solid. Bed sharing is just one of the ways a family can sleep together, but it is often chosen by nursing mothers. One of the biggest problems with bed sharing is safety.

Furthermore:

It is more dangerous for premature babies to share a bed, but they benefit greatly from sleeping close to their mother even if on a different surface.

Smokers must not sleep with infants;

The baby appears to be safer when sleeping next to the nursing mother;

Older siblings or other babies should not sleep with babies under the age of one year;

Very long hair must be tied up so that it does not twist around the baby's neck;

A parent who has exceptionally deep sleep or an extremely obese parent should consider not sleeping in the same bed with their child.

The American Academy of Pediatrics says, "Room sharing is recommended without bed sharing - this arrangement has been shown to reduce the risk of SIDS by up to 50%."

Some tips to improve your baby's sleep.

If you wish you can experiment with the advice below but remember that every family is unique as well as every child and what works for some does not work for others.

Observe your child, his temperament, also listen to your needs and then put into practice what you think is most suitable for the moment you are living!

Put your baby to sleep at the first signs of fatigue.

Timing is of the essence!

It is important to tune in to the baby's biological rhythms. In the evening, with fatigue, the levels of melatonin (from the 3rd month of life) in his brain are elevated and his body slips into sweet relaxation.

However, if you wait too long, your child will be too tired and his brain will start releasing stress hormones such as cortisol and adrenaline and melatonin levels will drop. This will make it difficult to fall asleep and may cause early awakenings.

So, pay attention to the signs of fatigue of the baby: when your little one is still, calm, disinterested in what surrounds him and looks into space, he is ready to sleep.

Eliminate the sound ... with sound (0 to 6 months).

A dark environment and a white noise machine muffle the noise and light from outside and make the environment look like a mother's womb.

Half of a newborn's sleep is REM sleep. The phase of light sleep in which it is very easy for even small noises to wake him up: your phone ringing in the living room, you talking too loudly, you dropping an object.

But this is less likely to happen if you use a white noise machine, because its sound will drown out any other noise.

Some have a timer, others stay on all night, and still others activate when the baby moves around in the crib.

White noise indicated for babies in the first months of life.

Swaddle the newborn (from birth until it begins to roll)

It is the ancient practice of wrapping the baby in a thin blanket to help him feel safe.

Also swaddling an over-stimulated baby helps him relax and calm excessive crying.

Whether you choose to swaddle your baby or not it is important to know the risks and benefits of this practice.

What are the benefits of swaddling the baby?

Your child will be less disturbed by the Moro reflex and therefore, by decreasing the jerks of arms and legs, he will be able to sleep longer.

Swaddling recreates that feeling of security your baby felt in your tummy when he had little room to move. Feeling "held" and wrapped up can help him calm down, so you may find that swaddling your baby helps him cry less.

What are the risks of swaddling the baby?

Experts recommend (if you are planning to swaddle your baby) to swaddle from birth. Otherwise, don't do it.

Stop swaddling your baby as soon as he shows signs of rolling on his side or tummy

If you practice co- bedding it is safer not to swaddle the baby, he could overheat

Do not cover the baby's neck or face with the sheet

If you decide to swaddle your baby, do it every time he sleeps, day and night, so that he becomes familiar with the feeling of being wrapped.

Relax your baby

During the first week of life, your baby will probably sleep for a long time, but after about two weeks, it may be more difficult for him to fall asleep so as soon as you see him sleepy or nervous, you can start calming him, rocking him, holding him. If you wait for him to moan, whine or cry, you are really late!

A child that is too tired will find it difficult both to fall asleep and to stay asleep! Newborns have short waking times as they tire easily! Watch your baby to intervene promptly when he shows the first signs of fatigue.

The movements of the mother cradle the baby as well as when he was in your belly.

In the first 3/4 months, babies need their mother near to fall asleep, it is a completely natural condition and must be indulged. Over time you will be able to propose new sleep strategies to your child, even overcoming the associations between external aids and sleep.

From around 6 months, these tips can create negative associations with your baby's sleep.

It is important for him to go to sleep the same way he will wake up throughout the night. If he wakes up briefly and you have "disappeared" or the movement has stopped he will wake up more and will have to call you to be "helped" once more.

You can only offer your baby new ways to fall asleep after 6 months of age.

Bright days / dark nights

Maybe you are tempted right away to always let your baby sleep in the dark to promote his sleep, actually to help him differentiate the day from the night, I recommend that you sleep in a room that is semi-dark during the day and dark at night.

Light is what prompts our eyes to tell us to stay awake even if it's time to sleep!

Routine is key.

If you have not yet started a bedtime routine, now is the time to do it: the evening ritual is perceived by the child as a reassurance.

Bedtime rituals that are always the same as themselves and gestures that are repeated day after day help the child to reach a state of relaxation that favors the onset of sleep.

We cannot teach our children to sleep, but we can accompany them in a serene way to this moment, which for them is abandonment and trust, cuddles and the scent of mum and dad.

The baby's routine.

A very simple and flexible routine reassures the child and gives parents a feeling of greater control over what they are experiencing.

It is not possible to establish rigid schedules, in the first months it is better to proceed slowly, get to know each other and understand what is best for the child and for you. It is important to be flexible with respect to feeding and bedtime times, however you can offer your child the same activities, in the same order, for example:

- ✓ Eat
- ✓ Stay a little awake (snuggle, change nappy, kick the cover)
- ✓ Sleep

About 10-20 minutes of activity may be enough. Some babies get tired after being awake for about 1.5 hours.

Always pay attention to your child's signs of fatigue, read his body language to see when it's time to stop the activity phase to put him to sleep.

Sleep from 4 to 11 months

At six months, the number of nocturnal feedings usually decreases significantly and many babies begin to sleep through the night; 70-80% will do so by nine months of age. When babies are put to bed and are sleepy but not asleep, they are more likely to be able to fall asleep independently even in the course of the night. Those who have not trained this ability will continue to ask for help from mom and dad to fall asleep. To acquire this ability, the support and presence of parents is essential.

Furthermore, during their development, children go through sleep regressions (4-8-12-18 months and 2-3 years). Regression describes a period of time when the sleeping baby suddenly begins to wake up at night, taking short naps and / or skipping naps for no apparent reason. Parents are often caught off guard by these changes. These are real growth spurts, moments in which the child is grappling with important achievements regarding his development, motor, cognitive and emotional.

Sleep at 1-2 years

Babies need around 11-14 hours of sleep. At around 18 months, they will take a single nap for about 1 to 3 hours. Naps should not be close to bedtime as they may delay falling asleep.

Towards the age of 2, the waking time gets longer, many children begin to remember their dreams better and are able to tell them, they also begin to have real nightmares.

On an emotional level, the child is facing important stages such as using the potty, moving to a bigger bed or to a room of his own, the arrival of a little brother or sister, entering the nursery.

Sleep from 3 to 5 years

Preschoolers sleep around 11-13 hours, and most don't take a nap after age five. As with young children, difficulties falling asleep and waking up during the night are common. With the further development of the imagination, preschoolers commonly experience night fears and nightmares. Additionally, sleepwalking peaks during this phase.

Some tips to improve your baby's sleep.

Put him to bed where he will have to spend the night

Often children are made to fall asleep on the sofa or in the bed and then moved to their crib, and this can confuse them: waking up at night in a different place than where they fell asleep, they may feel scared and disoriented, and all this will make it more difficult to fall back asleep.

Observe him in everyday life and spend time with him.

In this regard, any sleep difficulties and problems will give us a lot of information about the way he lives. We also consider that the more the child spends time with mom and dad during the day, the more he will be satisfied from this point of view and the less he will suffer from the "detachment" due to falling asleep.

Make good night a special moment

It should be time for you to interact with your child in a safe and loving, yet firm way.

Make sure your children have interesting and varied activities throughout the day, including physical activity and fresh air.

Don't fill your child's bed with toys.

The bed is a place to sleep, not a place to play. Too many toys in the bed can be distracting. One or two transitional objects - like a soft toy or a special book - are fine and can help him manage separation anxiety. Babies under 4-6 months of age should sleep in an empty crib to sleep safely.

Never threaten your child to send him to sleep if he is not behaving well.

Bedtime must be a safe, loving time, not a punishment. Your goal is to communicate to your children that it is good to go to bed, as it is for us adults. If the feeling of going to bed is a good feeling, the baby will fall asleep more easily.

Put him to sleep at the first signs of fatigue.

A very tired child is more irritable and nervous and therefore has more difficulty falling asleep. It is therefore preferable to avoid too turbulent or exciting games in the two hours preceding sleep.

Check the room temperature.

We all sleep better in a cool room. Try to keep the thermostat between 18-20 degrees.

Help him find the pacifier.

If your child wakes up because he has lost his pacifier, you can teach him where to find it: put a pair of pacifiers in the crib and every time he loses one at night, help him find it by guiding his hand to the corner where you placed it.

Is your child just born? Helps to program his " internal clock".

When babies are born, their internal clocks are out of sync with the external 24-hour cycle of daylight and darkness. It takes time for children to synchronize.

Thankfully, we don't have to passively wait for this to happen. In fact, we shouldn't be passive. Children depend on us for help.

Studies show that children adapt faster when parents give them the right environmental cues about the time of day.

Pay attention to television and other electronic media.

As already noted, nighttime use of electronic screens can cause problems because they emit anti-sleep artificial light.

Do you think your child is waking up? Be careful not to intervene too soon. Your baby may be asleep or ready to go back to sleep on his own.

The bedtime routine for older children.

Bedtime rituals that are always the same, and gestures that are repeated day after day help the child to reach a state of relaxation that favors the onset of sleep.

Always make the baby sleep in the same environment.

Choose the "right" moment, from an early age, each of us has a sort of internal biological clock that determines the rhythms of sleep and wakefulness.

Don't play rough games before going to bed.

At the first signs of fatigue, start your ritual.

Offer your child calm, quiet activities, such as reading, telling stories or singing lullabies, telling each other the most important events of the day.

If your child doesn't like some aspect of the bedtime routine, address that first. For example, if he doesn't like you brushing his teeth, do it immediately after his bath, not after reading two books and letting him snuggle quietly.

Always tell your child what you are / are doing, do it in a calm and relaxing voice, involve him in the things that are about to happen.

Below you can find some activities to include in your bedtime routine:

- ✓ take a bath
- ✓ put on pajamas
- ✓ brush your teeth
- ✓ go on the potty
- ✓ get a massage
- ✓ read a book
- ✓ sing a lullaby
- ✓ play a quiet game
- ✓ tell a story
- ✓ listen to music
- ✓ tell each other about the most important events of the day
- ✓ hugs and kisses.

Over time it is possible that the ritual is put to the test: "I have to go to the bathroom, I'm thirsty, another story, I'm afraid .. ". It is up to the parents to understand why this is happening in order to understand how to intervene.

Myths About Sleeping Babies.

Myth No. 1: if your baby is not sleeping, increase the amount of food! This will solve your difficult nights!

Baby's sleep is more complex than that! It is not enough to fill the baby's belly.

Food is a vital part of your baby's development, but weaning him won't be the solution to reducing nocturnal awakenings.

For babies over 4 months of age, sleep duration depends mainly on brain maturity and learned habits, less on the amount of food.

This does not mean that all babies over 4 months of age will sleep 12 hours, some may still require one, two or three more feedings. But overfeeding the baby before putting him to bed is probably not the way to go.

If you think your baby is waking up from hunger, you can try cluster feeding (offering more feedings before bed).

After six months, you may want to check his sleep patterns, habits and routines.

Here are some tips to improve your nights:

Consistent bedtime routine: Create a series of events that suggest to your baby's brain that sleep is on the way.

Sleep-Friendly Environment: Create a cool, dark room for comfort and relaxation.

Check that your child is not too hot, he may wake up often because he is thirsty!

Give him the opportunity to fall asleep independently: accompanying children to develop this ability is the basis for a more peaceful sleep.

Adequate Calories Throughout the Day: Offer breast or formula every 2.5-4 hours throughout the day based on your hunger stimuli. Sure, solids are important when the baby is the appropriate age, but your baby may still need milk.

Gradually reduce the number of calories at night so that your child consumes most of the calories during the day.

Myth No. 2: holding, cradling and carrying the baby are bad habits that will hinder your baby's sleep.

These methods are absolutely appropriate for the development of the little ones! There is no reason to feel guilty if your baby falls asleep in your arms. When you cuddle him and stay close to him, you set the stage for peaceful sleep.

Pampering for children is special ...

So special that some of you have spent the last 10, 20 or 30 years dreaming of holding your little one.

So special that some of you have spent 10, 20 or 30 thousand euros to have and hold your baby.

So special that some of you have been through loss after loss and that sweet baby in your arms is the sweetest balm ever.

So special that you are different after holding that precious life in your arms.

So why can others - people, books, experts, programs - make us feel like we're creating a bad habit just because we want to hold our babies? Keeping the baby in your arms is good! This is not the beginning of the end!

Myth No. 3: the melatonin myth: supplements that shouldn't be given to children.

Many parents turn to their pediatrician (when their baby is not sleeping well or enough) for help. The pediatrician, who often misses the many facets of sleep, recommends the use of melatonin.

Melatonin is a hormone produced by a gland at the base of the brain called the pineal gland or epiphysis and is considered the hormone responsible for the circadian sleep-wake rhythm in mammals. The release of melatonin is stimulated by the dark and inhibited by the light: for this reason, the secretion of the hormone increases progressively in the evening hours, reaches its peak during the night (between 2 and 4 am), falls to a minimum in the morning and remains very low during the day. In dark conditions, when the nerve cells of the retina are no longer affected by light, the epiphysis is stimulated to produce melatonin. Therefore, thanks to the secretion of this hormone, based on the alternation of light and dark, the sleep-wake rhythm is regulated in almost all living beings.

The brain of babies in the first three months of life does not produce melatonin and for babies there is therefore no difference between day and night! They often wake up day and night to feed themselves, be comforted, changed….

In a New York Times article earlier this year, Dr. Judith Owens, director of the Center for Pediatric Sleep Disorders at Boston Children's Hospital, said, "We don't know what the potential long-term effects of melatonin might be, especially when speaking of young children. Parents should know that the scientific evidence available is too limited to be able to define the real efficacy of melatonin in the insomnia of "healthy" children, ie those who simply struggle to sleep". In fact, melatonin should only be administered in cases of proven individual deficiency!

A study from the University of Maryland Medical Center suggests that at high doses melatonin can cause seizures and other research suggests that its use could potentially affect the development of the child's reproductive, cardiovascular, metabolic and immune systems and could be linked to premature puberty.

There is simply not enough evidence that melatonin supplements are safe for babies or children.

In short, it is not with pills that the sleeping issue is resolved but with understanding, practice and support. Mom and Dad can establish healthy sleep habits that benefit the whole family.

So, when daylight falls, I make sure that my baby is not subjected to strong lights, nor to the blue ones from tablets and TVs.

Turn down the lights in the house and encourage the natural process of his body!

Myth No. 4: To prevent your child from waking up too early, keep them awake longer!

They often say to you: “Your child goes to sleep too early”, which is said by those who either do not have children or who have them so old that they do not remember what babies need.

But the reality is based on science. A child who stays awake for too long becomes too tired, gets an extra dose of cortisol which makes relaxation more difficult.

Think about how you felt when you got ready to go out late on a Saturday night after a long day. Before going out, all you wanted was to get into your comfortable bed ... then instead you got ready, went out, your energy returned and the night turned out to be so explosive that you ended up dancing on the tables or something!!!

I can tell you from personal experience: Whenever I go to bed too late, I'm more restless and can't let go that fast. And I'm an adult! Imagine how a small child can feel!

Children should be put to bed when they show the first signs of fatigue, if we wait too long, they will have a return of energy which, however, will end with a lot of nervousness and at that point it will be more complicated to fall asleep.

Sleep aids concern one or more actions (for example, falling asleep at the breast or bottle, letting yourself be cradled, using certain rituals) that are useful for ensuring sleep for the baby.

Some modalities that seem adequate for a period, over time may be ineffective and affect the quality and continuity of sleep.

Let's take an example. A baby who falls asleep while breastfeeding finds suckling an effective way to relax. A fifteen-month-old baby, who continues to use breastfeeding to fall asleep, could remain "fixed" to this particular method of quieting and not have the opportunity to experiment with alternative comforting methods, even wanting more autonomy.

I realize that the subject can provoke many discussions and I would like to point out that no way of quieting is in itself "wrong" even when it comes to older children. The fact to keep in mind is that some aids, depending on the age, can affect the baby's sleep in terms of, for example, loss of continuity.

Obviously, there are two-year-olds who breastfeed and continue their sleep all night, without interruption, and some who are similarly lulled at bedtime and continue to sleep blissfully until morning. From experience, I admit that there are very few!

How to break some associations with sleep?

1. Vary the ways of accompanying sleep. A 3–4-month-old baby needs the help of the parent to fall asleep and it is difficult for him to be able to console himself on his own. At this age we can try to vary the ways of accompanying sleep, so that with growth it does not develop too strong an association with a particular way of falling asleep. We can, for example, arrange for him to fall asleep while walking in a sling or in the wheelchair, to fall asleep in the evening once with the feeding and once with the caresses.

2. Have the father intervene. Alternating between mom and dad in putting the baby to bed so that the child does not identify a single reference figure for sleep.

3. Gently detach the baby from the breast before he falls asleep. It is very easy and also completely normal for a baby, especially in the first months of life, to fall asleep while taking his feed. And for him and often also for his mother, there is nothing more pleasant. Sleeping and nursing is one of the fastest and most frequent associations. I would like to clarify that this is not a vice or a "bad habit", but simply a way that could consolidate over time. If we want to vary the ways in which the baby falls asleep, we can occasionally try to gently detach him from the breast before he falls into a deep sleep (this also in the first months of life). We can cradle him after feeding and then try to put him in the bed.

4. Separate the time of feeding from that of bedtime. Especially with older babies, tireless nocturnal feeders, it may be helpful to distance the time of the evening pre- sleep feed from the time you go to sleep. This means trying to anticipate the feeding by a quarter of an hour, half an hour and if it were possible to choose a different place than the bed and / or the room in which you sleep.

5. Cradle the baby without letting him fall asleep in his arms. Many babies learn to fall asleep in your arms, cradled. Also in this case, as for the feeding, an association could be established over time. To help the little one fall asleep alone without needing to be cradled, we can try to cradle him until he is almost asleep and then put him on the bed still conscious.

6. Respect gradual changes. When trying to change a habit or break an association with sleep, it is very important to be calm, gentle and patient. The principle is to respect the times of the child both considering the growth phase and the steps that are taken daily. Each child is unique, as is each period of his growth and also each parent is made in his own way. We consider all the factors that can influence and favor a change before setting ourselves goals that risk being unrealistic.

WE FOLLOW THE "TWO-WEEK TIME" RULE TO TRY TO MAKE A CHANGE. AFTER THIS PERIOD, LET'S TAKE STOCK, EVALUATE AND EVENTUALLY ADJUST THE SHOT!

www.ingramcontent.com/pod-product-compliance
Ingram Content Group UK Ltd.
Pitfield, Milton Keynes, MK11 3LW, UK
UKHW021915190726
13853UKWH00002B/682

9 798540 719025